THE READING ALOUD RESOURCE BOOK

This practical guide is the ideal tool for the busy practitioner or speech and language therapist to provide an effective, meaningful and contextualised approach to language development using picture books.

Drawing from up-to-date, evidence-based research, each chapter shows you how to get the most out of picture books to support language development, with a focus on the range of opportunities that reading aloud can bring. The guide offers a complete package to promote speech, language and early literacy, and to enrich language comprehension, vocabulary, phonological awareness and oral language – all by using books to provide a context for meaningful language learning. The resource also includes advice on how to develop intervention goals and outcome measures for reading aloud, with practical suggestions covering topics from creating a reading routine and book nooks, to encouraging reluctant readers and reading aloud challenges.

Language skills are essential for academic, social and communication success, and this reading aloud resource will be valuable reading for early-year educators, primary teachers, and speech and language therapists working with young children aged 0-7.

Katie Walsh and **Maria Bracken** are speech and language therapists and creators of Talking Buddies, a project to promote and foster language development in schools and communities. Together, they have almost 30 years' experience working with children with a wide range of communication difficulties.

THE READING ALOUD RESOURCE BOOK

A Practical Guide for Developing Speech and Language Using Picture Books

Katie Walsh and Maria Bracken

Routledge
Taylor & Francis Group

LONDON AND NEW YORK

Designed cover image: © Getty

First published 2023
by Routledge
4 Park Square, Milton Park, Abingdon, Oxon OX14 4RN

and by Routledge
605 Third Avenue, New York, NY 10158

Routledge is an imprint of the Taylor & Francis Group, an informa business

British Library Cataloguing-in-Publication Data
A catalogue record for this book is available from the British Library

Library of Congress Cataloging-in-Publication Data
Names: Walsh, Katie (Speech and language therapist), author. |
Bracken, Maria, author.
Title: The reading aloud resource book : a practical guide for developing speech and language using picture books / Katie Walsh and Maria Bracken.
Description: New York : Routledge, 2023. | Includes bibliographical references and index. | Audience: Ages 0-7 years | Audience: Grades K-1
| Summary:
-- Provided by publisher.
Identifiers: LCCN 2022054354 (print) | LCCN 2022054355 (ebook) |
ISBN 9781032202679 (Hardback) | ISBN 9781032202723 (Paperback) |
ISBN 9781003262961 (eBook)
Subjects: LCSH: Oral reading. | Picture books for children--Educational aspects. | Language arts.
Classification: LCC LB1573.5 .W34 2023 (print) | LCC LB1573.5 (ebook) |
DDC 372.6--dc23/eng/20221123
LC record available at https://lccn.loc.gov/2022054354
LC ebook record available at https://lccn.loc.gov/2022054355

ISBN: 978-1-032-20267-9 (hbk)
ISBN: 978-1-032-20272-3 (pbk)
ISBN: 978-1-003-26296-1 (ebk)

DOI: 10.4324/9781003262961

Typeset in Interstate
by Deanta Global Publishing Services, Chennai, India

Access the support material: https://resourcecentre.routledge.com/speechmark

CONTENTS

1 Introduction

> Reading for pleasure is the single biggest indicator of a child's future success – more than their family circumstances, their parents' educational background or their income.
>
> (Organisation for Economic Cooperation and Development, 2002)

Through our work as speech and language therapists (SLTs) in the Health Service Executive, we were seconded to work on a project which was sponsored by Sláintecare to promote speech and language skills in our local communities in Laois and Offaly. Sláintecare is a government-funded initiative to reform the healthcare system in Ireland. Through Sláintecare funding, we developed the Talking Buddies project. It was through the research for this project that we came to understand the rich opportunities that reading aloud can offer in terms of language development for children.

Our goal for the project was to develop language in the homes of as many families as possible, and we found that books were a quick and effective way to enrich the language environment of the home. Our aim was to support and target the language development skills of children aged 0–5 years.

In our experience, books are an under-utilised resource for the development of young children's language skills in the clinic room, the classroom and the home. We reviewed the literature regarding the potential benefits of reading aloud for a child's language development and we were extremely encouraged to find a large body of research boasting the benefits of reading aloud for all aspects of speech and language development.

As SLTs and teachers work with children whose language skills are delayed, picture books can be incorporated into treatment plans as a way to contribute greatly to the development of all areas of language (Wasik & Bond, 2001; Wesseling et al., 2017). This means that picture books could play a more central role for SLTs in the clinical setting. Similarly, picture books are a super resource for the classroom. While we are aware that many teachers read aloud to children during the school

DOI: 10.4324/9781003262961-1

day, they could also play more of a central role in the classroom, incorporating many of the learning outcomes outlined in the primary language curriculum.

Books are a resource that is widely available to all. Libraries offer fantastic services with options for ordering and renewing online, audiobooks and book recommendations. This means that books could and should be an important part of childhood education for all children. Language is the currency of education, and children with stronger language skills have a greater ability to access the curriculum and reach their potential. Books are an excellent way to promote language skills for all children. As SLTs, we want to promote books for all children in the community. In the words of Dr. Seuss (2019):

> the more that you read, the more things you will know,
>   the more that you learn the more places you'll go.

This book is aimed at professionals working with children aged 0–6 years.

The purpose of this resource book is to support people central to the child's life to use picture books in order to further develop speech and language skills. The book is applicable to SLTs, teachers of children aged 0–6, and anyone who is involved with the education of young children.

Background

Parents are a child's first teacher, and for small children, home is the best place to learn language. As SLTs, we are coming to a greater understanding of a parent's role in the development of the child's language skills. As the SLT profession gained a greater recognition of the unique relationship between the parent and the child, this led to a change in how SLTs provide services. This unique relationship can foster an optimal language-learning environment. Educating parents on how to create a language-rich environment in the home is becoming more of a priority for SLTs.

What does a language-rich environment mean? A language-rich environment is when the child's environment is full of great language models. The most common environments for children are homes, schools, homes of extended families and child-minding services. People closest to or surrounding the child play a crucial role in creating language-rich environments. This includes parents, teachers, child-minding carers and members of extended families.

When creating a language-rich environment, essentially we are trying to take every opportunity to use language, to interact, to teach and to share information and experiences. The good news is that it is not hard to provide a language-rich environment; it simply takes time and practice. The best part is that there is no need for expensive toys, tools or equipment!

We are experienced SLTs who have worked with children across a span of ages and speech, language and communication needs. Based upon experience and research, we feel there is a greater need for an emphasis on preventative interventions, whereby SLT services intervene to reduce the prevalence of developmental delays. The earlier the intervention, the better the outcome. The birth-to-3-year period has the fastest rate of brain development across our life span. A nurturing environment is crucial, not just for speech and language development but for overall brain development. We know that early intervention works but sometimes it's not provided to children at the right time, which for intervention is from the beginning. Imagine if parents and teachers had access to tools from the very start!

The goal of preventative interventions is to reduce the need for SLT referrals and to train parents and educators before any concerns about a child's speech, language or communication development arise. It's as straightforward as that! However, in reality, our model of service does not, at present, effectively facilitate preventative interventions. Preventative interventions ideally include training and education to the people in a child's life about how speech and language develops, milestones, referral pathways, intervention approaches and strategies. All this training would be supplemented with mentoring and coaching by the SLT. The reason this makes sense is that children need access to good language models. With education, parents, educators and other proximal people in a child's life can successfully improve children's language skills, particularly expressive language skills. The goal of this resource is to build personal and professional capacities that are supportive of young children acquiring age-appropriate language skills. This in turn should reduce the need for specialist SLT services for these children. As a consequence, the treatment duration required for the child should be reduced.

In Figure 1.1 below, we see how the child is placed in the wider context of their life.

Children's development is dependent upon the quality of interaction and support they receive within their environment. It is apparent that parents and teachers are present in their children's or pupils' everyday life. Consequently, educating, training and coaching teachers and parents is a largely effective way to support children both as a preventative or early intervention approach. This is a key point here. SLTs are simply not in a child's life the way that parents and teachers are. This means that we must upskill and educate those closest to the child.

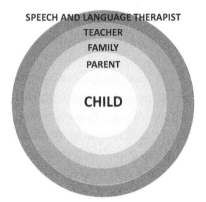

SPEECH AND LANGUAGE THERAPIST
TEACHER
FAMILY
PARENT

CHILD

Figure 1.1 Important people in a child's learning environment

Uniquely within the remit of a Speech and Language Therapist	Implementation of targets sitting with either the SLT or another person	Can and should be handed on
• Assessment • Goal setting • Intervention planning • Re-assessment • Educating • Coaching • Mentoring • Cohort Specialized Support (phonological disorder, stammering)	With the support of education, mentoring and coaching the implementation of an intervention plan as devised by a Speech and Language Therapist, can and should be, implemented at home and/or school.	• General language enrichment • Preventative intervention • Generalization of targets

Figure 1.2 Representation of competencies across the workforce

Let's look at Figure 1.2. This diagram (Malcomess, 2019) is based on Gascoigne's (2006) diagrammatic representation of the continuum of competencies in the workforce. Using Gascoigne's diagram, we can see how intervention may best be provided. This diagram suggests that educating people closest to the child is the most effective form of intervention. We used the diagram to map:

1. Roles that are uniquely within the remit of an SLT.
2. Roles that could be implemented by the SLT or another person in the child's life.
3. Roles that can and should be handed over to a person in the child's life.

This diagram demonstrates how parents and teachers are best placed to put language development strategies into practice. When these strategies are implemented every day, the child is in an optimum learning environment. The role of the SLT revolves around assessment, setting goals, educating, coaching and working directly with children who need specific interventions. SLTs are not with the child on a daily basis. By working jointly with teachers and parents, we upskill and educate those closest to the child. In this way, we create the best kind of language environment for children. This means a child gets timely intervention, provided in the right place at the right time. This is how we can prevent speech and language delays from occurring.

Both Figure 1.1 and Figure 1.2 indicate how there is much overlap between the roles of teachers and, of course, parents in the treatment of speech and language difficulties. Parents and teachers are already immersed in a child's life. We know from the research that children's speech and language develops within the context of their everyday life, experiences and environment. This is why it is crucial that those most proximal to the child are empowered with skills, resources and information that provide a language-rich environment.

Not only are these people most proximal to the child's everyday context and environment, but they are also more familiar to the child. Currently, in Ireland, for a child to receive speech and language therapy, parents must take children out of school and bring them to a clinic. By bringing speech and language therapy into the everyday environment and training people who are proximal to the child, we are reducing the need for this type of 'pull-out' service.

Figure 1.2 outlines how an SLT could safely delegate the delivery of interventions for a child. Particularly where there is a high level of competency in the child's context (e.g. at home or preschool), the SLT may be able to implement more of an advisory role where appropriate. Where the competency is less apparent or observed, then the main focus of the SLT would be to develop the competency in this environment. The key point that Gascoigne makes in this model of service is that the intervention is responsive to the child's needs and environment. In many circumstances, this means that intervention is provided and followed through in the child's everyday environment as opposed to in a clinical setting.

There is a cohort of our population that may be particularly vulnerable to delays – people who may not be as resourceful, able or curious. We need to consider the epidemiology of the population, such as those most at risk and those most likely to experience negative outcomes (Malcomess, 2019). It is well established in the literature that deprivation has a negative impact on language skills. Children from disadvantaged areas are at a higher risk of commencing school with language skills that are below average, significantly impacting their ability to learn to read, write and engage with the curriculum. Many families who are from lower socio-economic backgrounds struggle to access, let alone engage in, the services in their current form, and often these children fall through the cracks. If we look at our population and identify those most at risk, it is this cohort who have the greatest needs. They are more likely to struggle with language and literacy (Schwab & Lew-Williams, 2016), they have a greater likelihood of leaving school early and may also end up in the prison system (Chetty & Hendren, 2018). In fact, in a study completed by Bryan et al. (2015), up to 60% of young offenders have language difficulties yet these are the families who are less likely to access our service. These are often the families who need our services most, yet paradoxically they are least likely to access our services. Bringing language into the environment by training those closest to the child will make our services more accessible for these vulnerable families.

Teacher and SLT role

Parents, teachers and SLTs share many similar goals. While the SLT specialises in speech and language, the teacher's role is hugely significant in the child's life. Teachers are in a unique position to positively influence the child's language development. Teachers are with children daily throughout the school year and as a result build strong relationships. These types of bonds form the basis for language learning.

Our whole education system relies on language as its basis. The stronger the child's language skills are, the better they will perform in all areas of the curriculum. This leaves a lot of children at a distinct disadvantage. Teachers who feel confident identifying language weakness in the classroom and how to support these children are in a great position. This is the essence of a universal model and enables us, as SLTs, to have a much wider reach. Our current service, which is more specialised in nature, only captures those children who are specifically referred and have the capacity to access the service. The teacher, who is part of the child's daily life, is the best person to support the child's language skills. This is not to add another job to the teacher's ever-growing list of things to do. Children in a language-rich classroom are ultimately going to fare better as language imbues every aspect of the curriculum because it is a foundational skill. The stronger a child's language skills, the easier they can access all areas of the curriculum. Children attend school every week and being supported in this setting makes language intervention accessible and functional. In this model, children get intervention with the right person in the right place (Sláintecare, 2019).

To provide an example of the above, teachers are in a unique position to support language comprehension goals. For example, in our work we visited a local preschool that caters for children from the travelling community. Many of these children presented with significant language delays when we assessed them initially. Many of the children with delayed language were not accessing our service for various reasons. The preschool teacher was coached to reinforce new vocabulary from the weekly read-aloud. On one occasion, while reading *The Wonky Donkey* by Craig Smith and Katz Cowley, the teacher reinforced the word 'eyelashes', which many of the children were unfamiliar with. This book was repeated every day for a week so the children could hear this word often. The teacher also reinforced the word during playtime – for example, when the children were playing with dolls or other characters with eyelashes. During a later visit, the preschool teacher recalled how one child drew a picture and was excited to show her teacher the beautiful eyelashes she added to the drawing of her mother. This is simple to do but powerful for the children. Educating teachers and incorporating them into the intervention model of care to support language development is a highly effective way in which to improve language skills.

By homing in on a child's understanding and robustly teaching new vocabulary in any given topic, we will improve the learning outcomes in each and every subject and topic taught.

We need to teach language robustly. This means we provide language-rich information about each word. By equipping teachers with skills in the area of language development, they are in an ideal position to promote language development. A classroom needs to be a language-rich environment where the child's understanding and use of language are continually developing in a consistent and systematic way. This resource is a useful adjunct to support oral language development daily in the classroom.

2 Benefits of picture books

One of the easiest ways to imbue a child's life with rich language experiences is to read aloud to them every day. This is a relatively simple habit, and it can result in exponential benefits for the child's language development.

Studies show that the best 'toys' for developing language skills are real-life experiences and picture books (Sosa, 2016). This is exciting and an important message for every practitioner, teacher and parent to hear. Not only are books relatively cheap, but you can also access books for free from libraries!

Picture books are a fantastic resource to help with children's language development. Figure 2.1 depicts an infographic for how language develops. Reading aloud to children (especially from a very early age) has the potential to support children's learning at each stage – from the foundational level right up to the more complex skills such as expressive language and speech sound development.

In this chapter, we want to go into a bit more detail and highlight all the benefits there are to reading aloud regularly to children.

We all know that reading aloud to small children is beneficial and there is a wealth of picture books available on the market. However, for speech and language development specifically, we feel that books may be an under-utilised resource. Children love to hear stories read aloud, and this special time shared with an important other has enormous benefits for that child. The loving connection and interaction that occurs when we read aloud to children creates an environment that is optimal for language learning. For the parents, the experience of reading aloud to a child that culminates in them requesting 'read it again' shows the power of a great story to engage children. Once we have established the interaction, the stage is set for language learning.

Reading aloud supports brain development and bonding

The first benefit of picture books is that they contribute greatly to brain development. The first three years of life are a time of rapid brain development where neurons are firing and wiring together to form networks. It's never too early to begin

DOI: 10.4324/9781003262961-2

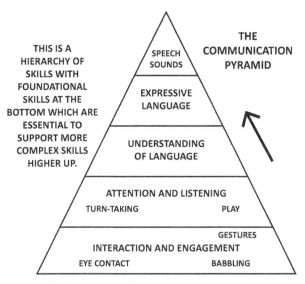

Figure 2.1 The Communication Pyramid

reading to a baby. In fact, some people even begin reading while the baby is still in the womb. Book sharing from birth is really just a time to connect with a new baby. Babies are soothed by the sound of their parent's voice, and at this stage it really doesn't matter what is read – it's the familiar sound of their parent's voice that seems to calm a baby in those early weeks. In the initial few months, a baby's vision is not fully developed, and this is why we see many high-contrast books, often black and white with single images on a page. This helps the baby focus on the object on the page. Reading to a baby from the very beginning sets up a cultural expectation that books are part of everyday life in the home.

Research by Dr John Hutton at Cincinnati University and published in *JAMA Pediatrics* in 2019 used MRI scans to analyse the brains of 69 preschoolers. The analysis showed that children who used screen-based media more had less-developed white matter in brain areas important for language and literacy than those who used screen media less. White matter is the insulated nerve bundles that criss-cross the brain and transmit information between different regions. Hutton went on to publish further studies that compared the use of screen time versus reading aloud on the child's brain. The results prove something that we already instinctively know: that reading aloud is great for children's brains. Now we have the MRI scans to prove it.

Reading aloud to babies in special care has been investigated for the potential positive effects on children who are separated from their parents. Having a baby in special care can be a very stressful time for a parent who cannot care for their child in the way they want to and cannot always enjoy the closeness of skin-to-skin contact.

Jain et al. (2021) show that reading aloud to babies in special care 'decreased parental stress, enhanced bonding, and supported positive parent-infant interactions'. Another 2021 study, by Neri et al., researched the possible advantages of reading books to preterm neonates on their subsequent language development. After preterm birth, infants are at high risk for delays in language development. This study showed positive effects on later language development and illustrates the positive effect sharing books with very young babies can have on bonding and early language development. Often it is not about the actual book but the experience of spending time with a loved one and sharing a pleasurable, joyful interaction. This sets the stage for positive attachment with the caregiver, which in turn is the basis for healthy social and emotional development and learning.

Sharing nursery rhymes with young children is a long tradition in our culture, and there is lots of evidence to back up the benefits of this practice. Nursery rhyme programmes on various websites and media are very popular with young babies and children. However, nursery rhymes on screen very much miss the point. The real beauty of a nursery rhyme is when it is read with a loved one. A parent can pace the timing of a nursery rhyme to keep the interaction going with the child; a screen cannot do this. Real language learning occurs in the security and love of an interaction where the parent will wait for the child to add in the last word such as 'Twinkle, twinkle, little...' or do the actions slowly for 'Head, shoulders, knees and toes'. Similarly, there are many websites and YouTube channels that read bedtime stories aloud. The benefit of this for very young children is limited in our opinion as optimum language learning occurs within responsive caregiver interactions. The difference between learning from screens and learning from real-life interactions with caregivers is that screens are no match for a person. Screens cannot respond contingently to the individual needs of our children (Cox Gurdon, 2019). So it can be said that reading aloud to children helps create a loving bond between parent and child. In the early years, building strong attachments to a loved one is an important basis for the child's development.

Reading aloud supports vocabulary development

Vocabulary skills are the hallmark of communicating one's needs, wants and emotions. The size and quality of a child's vocabulary are considered 'the bedrock' of language and early literacy skills (National Early Literacy Panel, 2008). In short, vocabulary growth is directly related to school achievement. I have countless examples of clients whose struggles with vocabulary impact their academic performance. This means that those whose vocabulary skills are significantly impaired compared to classmates will experience less academic success. As education is predominantly taught through language, it is reasonable to conclude that any child who is experiencing language difficulties is going to see a knock-on effect, however great or small, on their academic achievements. Vocabulary is the foundation of language, and language is the main instrument we use in all cultures and nationalities across the world for learning skills, communicating, socialising and more. The extent of a child's vocabulary knowledge at age 3 is predictive of the child's future academic success (Hart and Risley, 2003).

What does vocabulary mean?

The number of words that you know determines your vocabulary bank. The Oxford Dictionary (2023) defines vocabulary as 'all the words a person knows or uses'. Vocabulary knowledge includes both vocabulary breadth and depth. The breadth of vocabulary knowledge refers to having at least surface-level understanding of lots of vocabulary words. For example, I have heard the word 'sagacious' before and I know that it relates to wisdom or having good judgement, but I am not sure I could use the word effectively in written or oral language. This suggests that I have a surface-level understanding of the word. On the contrary, depth of vocabulary suggests a full, rounded understanding of a word. For example, my knowledge of a synonym of 'sagacious' such as 'wise' or 'shrewd' is robust, and I can confidently say I could use both words effectively in writing or conversation.

This is an important factor to consider when teaching children new vocabulary. We cannot expect children to use new words automatically in their own talking or writing if they do not robustly understand the word (i.e. vocabulary depth). Children can only use new words effectively when they are exposed to all the elements that relate to this word many times, in different contexts. For example, we need to focus on developing:

- the semantics of this word (what this word means and how it relates to other words)
- the phonology of this word (how this word sounds when spoken aloud)
- the orthographic (how this word looks when written down)
- the syntax (the grammar rules that accompany this word).

Speech and language therapists (SLTs) have a great interest in vocabulary as words are the primary way in which young children communicate their needs. Vocabulary development begins from the very first time a child hears a word and begins to connect this pattern of sounds with something in their environment. Every time the baby hears the word 'dada' spoken in his environment or spoken to him, and also has the opportunity to see his father in his environment, he is beginning to link this word to his father and thus begins his early vocabulary development. Generally speaking, at around 9–12 months of age babies say their first word; by age 2, we expect a child to say about 50 words. However, the number of words they understand is far higher.

Everyone in a child's life should feel empowered to teach their child/student new vocabulary during everyday interactions. This level of empowerment is not, and should not be, reserved just for professionals such as SLTs or educators. Anyone present in a child's daily life plays a critical role in supporting their language and vocabulary. This means that parents, siblings, grandparents, childminders and extended family should all be empowered by the level of support they offer a child every day.

It's in the simple, everyday interactions that a child learns the most. Recently, I read aloud to a little 4-year-old boy, called Luke, whose language skills in conversation were age-appropriate – in fact, advanced for his age. We sat side by side, looking at a picture book together. I followed his lead and commented about what he was looking at or interested in, and our time together turned into a conversation about the book. From this brief interaction with him, I exposed him to two new words on one page. The two words were 'perched' and 'content' (happy). The strategies I used supported his interest, attention and understanding. I made comments that extended beyond what he could physically see in the pictures. I asked questions that got him thinking beyond what he could see. I related the word to his everyday life. I explained the meaning of the word and talked about words that were related to it and differed from it. I worked towards building his 'lexicon', which refers to the semantic understanding of the word and how he stores the word in his brain. An analogy of a strong semantic system is a tidy filing cabinet or a wardrobe! The more categories and subcategories are employed to organise the contents of the cabinet, or the more groups clothing items are organised into, the easier it is to find that document or that elusive 'nice top' that goes with your good pair of jeans. The more disorganised the system, the harder it is to find that 'nice top'. The same is true for vocabulary: the more organised the storing of vocabulary in our lexicon, the easier it is to access and use. If a child's semantic system is weak, we will see difficulties in word retrieval and processing, and errors in their associations about functions/ uses/synonyms/antonyms. In-depth understanding of vocabulary is very important for learning to use new vocabulary appropriately.

Later on, as little Luke was tidying up to go home with his mother, he said, 'Look, my hat is perched on the chair!' While this child did not have any language difficulty and had an eagerness to learn new words, it anecdotally demonstrated how simple interactions such as sharing a book together gave Luke an opportunity to learn new words. We shared a book together; the context and the learning situation were so simple! The interaction was relaxed, fun, engaging and almost conversational.

The vocabulary in picture books is widely different to the vocabulary we use in conversation. Vocabulary found in books is more academic, descriptive and formal than the language we use in everyday social interactions. So one of the main benefits of reading books with children is that books offer an opportunity to hear vocabulary that does not come up in everyday interactions. A wide-ranging vocabulary enables better communication, better understanding and, later better reading and writing. The lexical diversity in books is clearly shown by Gillam and Ukrainetz (2006) in their 'Goldilocks' example which shows the difference between the conversational language we would use to tell the story of Goldilocks and the literate language that we would read in the text.

Conversational language

Goldilocks walked down the road and she saw the bear's house. She knocked on the door. Nobody answered, so she looked in. She saw some bowls of soup on the table so she sat down to eat.

Literate language

A little girl named Goldilocks was walking down the road when she saw the house where the three bears lived. After knocking very loudly on the door a few times, she opened it up very quietly and peeked in. As she stepped into the kitchen, she noticed three hot steaming bowls of soup on the table. She was very hungry, so she went for the biggest bowl that belonged to the papa bear.

We can see that the literate language is far more sophisticated in terms of vocabulary and syntax. The authors write: 'Literate language tends to be decontextualized, more abstract, and more formal than conversational language… Vocabulary choices within literate language tend to include diverse, abstract, multisyllabic, and sophisticated words.' When we read aloud to children, we are inputting sophisticated language patterns and vocabulary into their brains. Sarah Mackenzie, author of *The Read-Aloud Family* (2018) and host of the Read-Aloud Revival podcast, tells us that picture books are designed to be read aloud by adults, so the language in them is often more complex and diverse than in early novels. This view is reiterated by Montag, Jones and Smith; in their 2015 study, they ask the question 'What do early picture books provide that everyday conversations may not?' They examined more than 100 books and compared them to conversation samples. They found greater lexical diversity in books compared with child-directed speech and concluded that 'shared book reading creates a learning environment in which infants and children are exposed to language that they would never have encountered via speech alone'.

Kate Nation is an experimental psychologist and expert on language and literacy development in children. She and her colleagues recently published an article entitled 'Book language and its implications for children's language, literacy and development' (Nation et al., 2022). In this study, the authors review the nature and content of children's book language and conclude that exposure to books affords children the opportunity to learn 'words and syntactic constructions that are only rarely encountered in speech and that, in turn, this experience drives further developments in language and literacy'. The authors also highlight that the range, variety, depth and sophistication of language in books promote children's social and emotional development.

It's important that reading aloud is incorporated into the home environment to supplement a child's language-learning environment. A language-rich environment is the goal, and it's this kind of environment that will build a child's vocabulary. Many of you will be familiar with the '30 million word gap'. For those who aren't, it was a study completed by Hart and Risley (2003). They assessed 36 children in lower, middle and upper socio-economic homes. From their research, they discovered that children in lower-income families hear 30 million fewer words than children from higher-income families by the time they are 3 years old. In higher-income families, there is a greater likelihood of the child being immersed in a more sophisticated and language-rich environment. They discovered that children in welfare families had a vocabulary of 525 words, whereas children in higher socio-economic families had a vocabulary of 1,116 words. They also discovered that, at age 3, children will be exposed to 4,662 words if they were never read to, 63,570 words if they were read to 1-2 times per week, 169,520 words if they were read to 3-5 times a week; 296,660 words if they were read to daily; 1,483,300 words if they heard five books a day (Hart & Risley, 2003). Hart and Risley completed a follow-up of these children's language skills and were 'awestruck' when they discovered that the assessments they completed at age 3 accurately predicted later language skills at ages 9-10. In summary, the vocabulary skills of children at 3 years of age are predictive of later academic success (Hart & Risley, 2003).

Despite some criticism of Hart and Risley's findings, their study does provide some important information. It highlights the importance of parent/child interaction and the benefits of reading aloud to children. Moreover, it reinforces how critical the early years are for language development and preparing children for printed text in schools. It shows us the importance of our language models and interactions in supporting children's language skills. A language-rich environment is essential for language development.

If we examine the popular children's book *Peepo* by Janet and Allan Ahlberg – a classic! – it is filled with fantastic vocabulary, so much so that this 'baby' book is appropriate for children way past the formative first five years! How many 3-, 4- or 5-year-old children do you know who use the words 'tassel', 'fringe', 'squabbling' or 'dozing' in their own speech? I do not doubt that some do have this vocabulary. However, the point is that this is just an example of the great vocabulary in this book that many 3–5-year-old children will not understand or use in their own talking. Interestingly, this type of vocabulary could very well come up later on in school, and they may not have the understanding of these words – when we expect them to – if they are not exposed to this language in vocabulary-rich environments from a young age.

Reading aloud has the power to support the language development of all children, not only children who have speech and language difficulties. The beauty of reading aloud is that it can be done by anyone in a child's life, not just an SLT or an educator. This means that anyone in a child's life can feel empowered to support their child's language learning, once they know a few tips and tricks to get the most out of the reading-aloud experience.

Reading aloud supports attention and listening skills

Attention and listening skills are essential for the child to be able to engage with others, understand spoken language and respond contingently. This is the foundation for language and later literacy, and, as we can see in the Communication Pyramid, they form the basis for all subsequent language learning. Initially, children learn to pay attention to an important other such as a parent who gazes into their eyes and smiles. The child next learns to attend to an object such as a mobile above his head. Joint attention, which emerges between 6–12 months, is the ability to shift the attention between the object and the person. This is integral to language social and cognitive development. It is often one of the first things we notice in children who are on the autistic spectrum. From here, attention skills develop more and more, allowing the child to attend for increasing lengths of time. According to *Jim Trelease's Read-Aloud Handbook*, 'the best tool for expanding attention span is one-on-one time with a child' (2019). Books are a brilliant way to spend this time; they are colourful and engaging and have characters that appeal to young children. Jim says that attention and listening develop page by page, book by book. Children who aren't often exposed to books cannot be expected to attend for more than a fleeting glance at a joy that is unknown to them.

What can therapists and teachers do to support the development of attention and listening skills in the child?

1 Encourage a daily reading routine in the home. Start where the child is at and use short, fun, engaging books, gradually building up to longer and longer texts.
2 Select good-quality books and encourage parents to do the same. This will keep the child engaged for longer.
3 Follow the child's lead in terms of their interests as this will help develop their attention and listening. Motivation is key. Some parents have told us that they

found it difficult to get their child interested in story books, but by using non-fiction books in their specific area of interest, they managed to get their child interested and motivated for storytime. Often non-fiction books will target specific areas of interest and encourage the child to listen for longer about a topic of interest. So whether the child is interested in dinosaurs, princesses or nature, there is a non-fiction book to keep them engaged. Many non-fiction books have interactive flaps to lift, which keep the child engaged for longer. For example, Usborne's *How Things Work* is a fascinating book for children interested in machines and the details of their levers, cogs, pulleys and coils. The bright, bold illustrations, coupled with the sturdy flaps, will easily draw an interested child in and keep their attention and listening for longer.

4 Many of the modern classic stories have 'big book' versions available and this can help to draw the child in as the illustrations are larger and clearer and can be more easily explored and discussed. These books are ideal for an educational setting.

5 Depending on the child's unique sensory profile, they may need more movement or sensory stimulation in order to listen for longer. We don't need children to sit robotically with quiet hands to benefit from storytime. For some children, having a fidget toy in their hands or listening to a story while doing some Lego can help maintain and develop their attention and listening.

6 Choose books that are appropriate to the child's language ability. It is particularly important that the book you read is not at too high a level because this will immediately cause the child to lose interest. Having to stop multiple times to explain challenging words that come up can make it difficult for the child to make sense of the narrative. If you find the book is too challenging for the child and they are losing interest, you can always talk about the pictures and simplify the text as you go.

7 Consider the topic of the book and whether the child has any personal experience or background knowledge of this. A child might benefit from learning some vocabulary about sea creatures before hearing the story of *The Snail and the Whale* by Julia Donaldson and Axel Scheffler.

8 Use your voice to stress key words and to help keep the child engaged. Different character voices also help bring the story to life. The reader's familiarity with the book is important here. By familiarising yourself with the story beforehand, you can read the story with a better sense of the flow of the narrative and the intonation required for the story.

Reading aloud supports grammatical development

Grammar is a set of rules for how words, phrases and sentences are combined. As soon as children have a small bank of works, they begin combining words to form short phrases, and this is the beginning of grammatical development. A small child might say 'Mammy up' to communicate her needs and, as her vocabulary develops, so too does the complexity of her language. This allows the child to express more sophisticated ideas and share more complex details. Parents and educators play a critical role in facilitating grammatical development by modelling correct grammar and sentence structure. They promote grammatical development by modelling grammar of increasing complexity, thereby stretching the child into their 'zone of proximal development' (Vygotsky, 1978).

Here are the milestones for grammatical development:

- **12-18 months**: The child will begin to use first words.
- **18-24 months:** The child will begin to combine words to make short phrases. They then will begin to use word endings such as 'ing' as in 'jumping'.
- **2 years:** The child will use plurals such as 'blocks' and past tense such as 'kicked' and later irregular past tense such as 'ran' and possessive 's' such as 'mammy's coat'. The child will begin to use early pronouns such as 'my', 'mine', 'I', 'she', 'he', and ask simple questions such as 'who', 'what', 'where'.
- **3 years:** The child will start saying longer sentences of 3+ words, sentences with more than one verb such as 'I want to play on the swing', and more complex questions such as 'when', 'why' and 'how'.
- **3-4 years:** The child will begin to say full sentences with function words such as 'the', 'a', 'is' and 'does': 'Boy eat ice cream now' → 'The boy is eating ice cream now'. This child also begins to join two sentences: 'I went to the park and saw the ducks.' Other conjunctions such as 'because', 'before', 'if', 'so' and 'like' also emerge.

Children's grammar will develop as they are exposed to lots of language. The kind of language we use is also important. We must offer children language-rich learning opportunities. To do this, educators can employ a variety of strategies such as expanding upon children's language, modelling complex language and talking explicitly about words, phrases and sentences.

Picture books provide an easy way to expose children to more sophisticated language patterns and grammar. Not only will picture books help to expose children to language-rich experiences, but they also offer the communication partner the opportunity to model the same. As children hear stories read aloud, they are hearing complex grammar and sophisticated sentences. Children love to hear stories again and again, and this repetition can work to teach and generalise the grammatical rules of the language.

Let's describe a situation where grammar skills can be supported through sharing picture books. Let's say a child is confusing his pronouns and incorrectly using the pronoun 'he' instead of 'she'. His awareness and use of 'she' will be greatly helped by *hearing* books with a female character. For example, in the book *Rosie Revere, Engineer* by Andrea Beaty, the word 'she' is used on every page: 'Alone in her attic, the moon high above, dear Rosie made gadgets and gizmos *she* loved. And when *she* grew sleepy, *she* hid her machines, far under the bed, where they'd never be seen.'

Similarly, a child struggling with irregular past tense would greatly benefit from hearing books with lots of irregular past tenses such as *Zog* by Julia Donaldson and Axel Scheffler, which includes a wide variety of irregular past tense verbs. For example:

- Madam Dragon *ran* a school
- She *taught* young dragons
- Then up and off he *flew*
- Now that you've *been* shown
- His throat *grew* hoarse
- He *blew* with all his might
- Nursed them when they *fell*

The beauty of the book is that it is an enjoyable experience for the child with no pressure on the child to answer questions. The first step in learning any part of language is to expose them to what we want them to learn. Helping to support children's grammatical constructs is achieved in the same way. Exposing the children to grammatical rules through reading aloud subtly develops their language as these rules are inputted day after day as the story is repeated. In a local preschool we visited, the preschool teacher remarked that many of the children struggled with the 'she' pronoun. By reading the story of *The Dinky Donkey*, the teacher could reinforce the use of the correct pronoun. '*She* was so cute and small, *she* had beautiful long eyelashes, *she* loved to listen to rowdy music, *she* painted her hooves bright pink, *she* had to go pee pee, and *she* loved to play the piano'. Repetition of the story is always important. For some children, more explicit teaching of these grammatical structures may be required, and this can be done simply by talking about the story and encouraging the child to retell parts of the narrative. In this situation, when they use incorrect grammar, we can recast or say it the correct way, or we can say: 'Rosie Revere is a girl, we use "she" for a girl.' Completing different types of extension activities after the read-aloud in a classroom or preschool context could also help to reinforce the learning of the pronoun 'she'.

Reading aloud for social and emotional development

While we have already talked about how reading aloud supports attachment and bonding in the early years, as the child develops, reading aloud continues to support the child's social and emotional development. Pam Leo is a literacy activist, founder of the Book Fairy Pantry Project and author of the international best-selling book *Connection Parenting*. During her research, Pam came across a shocking statistic that two-thirds of the 15.5 million children living in poverty in the U.S. do not have even one book to call their own. Pam set about changing this by collecting gently used books and dispensing these books at food pantries. This became the Book Fairy Pantry Project. We interviewed Pam and she explained to us why she believes reading aloud is so important for small children. Pam states that 'only the children with books can read, and only the children who can read can thrive'. Children, she says, often struggle at night to settle to sleep. What they really need is for their emotional cup to be filled up after the day. Reading aloud works to fill their emotional cup with the connection that they need so that they can fall asleep with ease. Reading aloud is a wonderful way to build social and emotional skills such as confidence, self-esteem and connection.

Reading aloud also supports the child's ability to empathise with others. In her book *The Read-Aloud Family*, Sarah Mackenzie speaks about the power of stories to help children walk a mile in another's shoes: 'Stories, it turns out, are incredible empathy builders, the process of entering into a life different from our own compels us to see the world from another point of view' Mackenzie (2018, p.77). A study by Kurtts and Gavigan (2008) also tells us how books can be an effective way of promoting inclusion and developing empathy for minority groups, such as in disabled cohorts:

> The use of children's literature is a way to share powerful examples of how we all may or may not relate to individual differences. This can be especially true for understanding how disabilities impact the lives of individuals and their families and friends. For preschool teachers, exposure to children's literature about disabilities is an effective instructional tool for helping students develop empathy and understanding of diversity, but also to inform their own professional practice as they prepare to meet the individual educational needs of children in their classrooms as well as in practice.
>
> (Kurtts & Gavigan, 2008)

Children's Books for Wellbeing, published in 2020 by the Professional Development Service for Teachers, is an excellent resource that looks at the value of books to support social and emotional wellbeing. The authors state:

> Stories can humanise abstract issues and encourage children to think and talk about how they might feel and what they might do in a particular situation. Books about sensitive issues can be used in the classroom to promote discussion and complex thinking among children, as they examine problems and explore possible solutions.

Reading aloud supports narrative development

Reading aloud also supports the child's ability to tell stories for themselves. Communicating with other people in our world is all about sharing our own story. We talk about what happened in the schoolyard or an incident at a birthday party. The skill of retelling a story which follows a logical sequence with a beginning, middle and end does not always come naturally to children. In speech and language sessions, therapists spend a lot of time helping children to understand how to retell a story, and this is sometimes a real struggle. Children leave out important information and end up telling you the end of the story without giving you important details such as who, what, where, the problems and the solutions. This leaves the listener confused, forced to ask the child to rewind and answer a lot of questions! Reading stories aloud provides the child with an excellent model of good story structure. Each time the child hears a story read aloud, he hears a story with a beginning, middle and end. This promotes knowledge of story structure and the components of a good story.

One type of book that can really support the child's narrative development is the wordless picture book. Wordless picture books are books that have very few or no words and the story is told through the illustrations. The beauty of these books is that the story can be told by anyone regardless of literacy level or language. Without the printed words, the adult and child are much more likely to engage in dialogic reading and the book becomes more of a two-way conversation with both talking about what they see and notice in the illustrations. This has been shown to be a wonderful way to learn new vocabulary.

Wordless picture books are also a wonderful way to share a book with families who do not speak the dominant language in the community. In 2012, the International Board on Books for Young People (IBBY) Italy launched a project called Silent Books which used wordless picture books to harness the power of narrative and bridge linguistic and cultural barriers for the many refugees landing on the shore of the island of Lampedusa in Italy. Author Rose Marie Lindfors writes that 'Storytelling is a historical and traditional pastime and is something we share with all of humankind across the globe' (Lindfors, 2016, p.7). The silent books helped to reach out to people of all cultures regardless of the language they spoke, created meaningful connections and shared experiences, and sparked a desire to learn a new language and to read. The project was so successful that it is now being spread all over the world.

As SLTs, we love to promote wordless picture books because of the fantastic opportunities there are to develop language skills, boost vocabulary and strengthen our ability to attend and listen to a story. Wordless picture books can also offer the opportunity for the child to tell the story back in their own words, giving them a chance to practise their storytelling skills and practise important narrative skills. Learning the structure of a story – beginning, middle and end, what happened first, next, last – helps the child learn how to structure a story and in turn improves their own narratives and, in time, their writing skills.

Wordless picture books are also a great way for autistic children to develop their problem-solving and inferencing skills. Some children can read well but struggle with a comprehension piece. Wordless picture books force them to think about the story and figure out the meaning to make sense of the story. This helps them to think more figuratively. 'It's a radical decision not to use words,' wordless picture book creator David Wiesner (2021) tells us. 'When the artist removes the text, they invite readers to decode the pictures for themselves.' Wordless picture books are powerful tools for children with learning differences.

Reading aloud supports literacy development

Reading picture books aloud is beneficial not only for language development but also for later reading and literacy success. As children's author Mem Fox describes, 'Once children have masses of rhythmic gems in their heads, they'll have a huge store of information to bring to the task of learning to read. A nice fat bank of language; word phrases, structures and grammar'.

All of this exposure to language is supportive of later reading success. Within our professional working life, quite often parents communicate the difficulties their children face with literacy skills in school. Before we embarked on a deep dive into the research on picture books for supporting language development, we largely considered literacy-based concerns to be the concern of the teacher, which they are. However, some of the key components of literacy success include language comprehension, vocabulary knowledge, syntax, semantics and phonological awareness. These are very much within the remit of the SLT. We already knew that picture books are effective in supporting speech and language skills. This is clearly identified in the literature. However, another benefit of reading picture books aloud is the essential role this plays in later literacy success.

Traditionally, SLTs target the language work and the teacher's role is more focused on phonics. However, both professions should be taking a more holistic view of how language and literacy are inextricably linked and how literacy develops.

The reading rope is an infographic proposed and created by Dr Hollis Scarborough (2001). The reading rope, as can be seen below, describes the complexities involved in learning to read. It consists of upper and lower strands. The upper strands include background knowledge, vocabulary, language structures, verbal reasoning and literacy knowledge. These strands become increasingly strategic with practice and instruction. The lower strands include phonological awareness, decoding and sight recognition of familiar words. These strands become more automatic with practice. All of these strands interconnect, and learning in each strand does not necessarily happen in isolation. Learning, therefore, does not happen overnight but rather happens with time, exposure and practice.

What is the role of language comprehension in learning to read?

As can be seen in Figure 2.2, there are many strands that relate solely to that of language. Language skills make up a huge proportion of literacy skills. For children to understand and make sense of the text in sentences or paragraphs, they need first to have a background context. This means they need to have some background information and content about a topic so that they can understand what is being read. So how do we do that? We need to immerse children in all the vocabulary that relates to an idea or topic. We need to develop their semantic systems to understand how ideas and words interact, relate and differ. We need to help them understand concepts, share facts and predict or infer meaning. Essentially, background knowledge is developed through language. Comprehension of content around a topic is a slowly developing process. We have to give children enough time to learn more about what they are reading to give them the best chance at reading comprehension and, in turn, literacy skills.

Once you delve deeper into the theory of how literacy develops, it can provide some context or reason for why children may be struggling to read. The reading rope is a useful guide to help understand these challenges. Even if the child has an adequate level of decoding or word recognition ability, the level of word knowledge and background knowledge they have can impact their success in interpreting a passage or a reading piece. The prime indicator of a child's success in school is

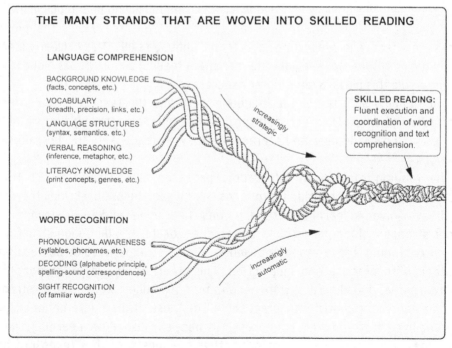

Figure 2.2 The reading rope. (Scarborough, 2001)

how many words the child knows. While children do attend school to learn new words, their vocabulary knowledge prior to starting school and during the early school years will determine how much of what the teacher says is understood. In the context of reading, reading skills are dependent upon language skills. Reading also depends upon phonological awareness and other skills within the reading rope (Scarborough, 2001).

Children can only successfully achieve skilled reading abilities if all strands of Scarborough's reading rope are activated and supported. Children with good learning potential can do this with little effort, but they will almost always benefit from a whole-system, systematic approach to skilled reading. However, children who have difficulties such as dyslexia or language delays or disorders will need more input. While the basic strategies for reading comprehension are sufficient for most (such as re-reading the text, asking questions about the story or encouraging the child to summarise the story), some children require more support. These comprehension strategies will simply not be enough for the child if that child does not have background knowledge – the facts or vocabulary about the topic. It is these language-based components that bolster a deep understanding of a topic and consequently support reading comprehension. Without background knowledge and the language that makes the text come to life, the text is meaningless. Naturally, repeatedly asking children to engage in reading comprehension activities that are above his/her level of comprehension will be demoralising, demotivating and impactful on their self-esteem.

Jim Trelease explains that, for some kids, background knowledge is acquired by visiting museums, zoos and historic sites, travelling abroad or camping, among many other experiences. Aside from travelling and being exposed to many different experiences from a young age, he also explains how the best way to gain background knowledge is by reading or being read to. The majority of people do not have the luxury of extensive holidays and explorations with children, so it is encouraging to know that there is something we can do to extend their knowledge and learning. For those children who have been exposed to and gathered background knowledge, they are fortunate to be in a position to bring extensive information to the learning table. Let's imagine a typically developing child who has been lucky enough to visit the National Museum. He got to explore the museum, attend the tours and experience different artefacts. It's reasonable to conclude that he will almost definitely do better on a comprehension task about Irish history compared to a typically developing child who never had the opportunity to visit the museum. Most year groups have children who are not from the same socio-economic background; quite often, there is a huge variation in each year group. We need to be mindful of this as we introduce new topics. Is there anything that can be done to build up the comprehension, vocabulary and background knowledge of those children who have had fewer learning opportunities? This is where exposure to books and educational videos is critical.

Educators play a key role in supporting language as they, like parents, are immersed in the child's environment. An environment rich in language is a key factor in aiding children to reach their language-learning potential. Creating a language-rich environment is straightforward once you know how. Incorporating books into the child's everyday experience is a great place to start. Books offer lots of opportunities to hear different language components, which we explain further in the next chapter.

In summary, reading aloud to children supports vocabulary development, attention and listening, grammatical development, social and emotional development, literacy and narrative development. However, it is more than the sum of its parts and the benefits are exponential. Children who hear stories read aloud regularly have stronger language skills, and the benefits are far-reaching.

Children with strong language skills have a love of learning, curiosity and an appetite for further learning. These children can easily problem-solve and predict problems in their environment. The general format of a storybook is: introduction, problem, overcoming the problem and conclusion. By reading aloud to children day after day, we model how they can overcome the problems they face in their own lives. The ability to generalise an experience to your own life is a skill and one that books enable us to develop with exposure and practice.

Children's ability to empathise with characters in books builds empathy for others around them and the world they live in. Language helps children understand themselves and their world in a deeper and more meaningful way. Reading provides a foundation for language and all other learning. This platform opens the child's eyes to experiences, information, perspectives and cultures that give a child a higher level of cognitive functioning compared to those not exposed to books.

3 How to use picture books to support language

Language components in picture books

To get the most out of books for supporting language development, it is essential that we know the kind of language that we find in books. This knowledge helps us to identify what might be the best language targets for a child so that we can individualise goals for them. Vocabulary includes many elements of language, and some elements of language are more difficult to learn than others. Learning nouns is the easiest type of vocabulary to learn. This is because nouns are concrete and visual. Let us walk you through the language you will find in books in the hope that this knowledge will help you set appropriate goals for children.

- **Nouns:** These are words used to identify people, places and things. Examples: dog, Paris, Wednesday. Early picture books for the very young have a noun on each page helping children to become familiar with basic objects.
- **Verbs:** These are words that describe actions and are commonly also referred to as 'action words'. Verbs are the only type of word that are absolutely necessary to make a sentence. This is why verbs are crucial for budding talkers as it's through their knowledge and use of verbs that children can make and expand sentences. Children with developmental language disorder (DLD) quite commonly struggle with verbs, which in turn significantly affects their ability to make sentences.
- **Grammar:** This is the ability to combine words to formulate sentences. Picture books are full of rich grammar and sentence structures.
- **Pronouns:** A pronoun is a word that you use to refer to someone or something when you do not need to use a noun. Examples: I, you, he, she.
- **Past tense (regular):** The simple past tense shows that you are talking about something that has already happened. Regular past tense follows the same pattern. Examples: jumped, watched, cleaned.

DOI: 10.4324/9781003262961-3

- **Past tense (irregular):** Irregular past tense verbs are verbs that do not form their past tense by adding 'ed' to the end of the word. Examples: ate, caught, wrote.
- **Present tense:** This tense includes 'ing' endings. In the active voice, the subject in the sentence is performing the action. Example: I am doing my homework.
- **Adjectives:** These are words that describe the qualities or states of being a noun. Examples: enormous, tiny, amused. Quality picture books will use lots of descriptive adjectives that sometimes children won't hear in everyday conversations.
- **Concepts:** They are words that describe abstract ideas. Picture books are a great way to develop comprehension of early concepts. Examples include:
  - Emotions: happy, sad, frustrated, elated
  - Qualitative: big, little, enormous
  - Quantitative: more, less
  - Positional: in, out, on, under
  - Temporal: first, then, last, before, after
  - Colour, shape, size
  - Characteristics: empty/full, asleep/awake, new/old

All of the parts of language are represented in children's books. As mentioned previously, the language in books can often be more sophisticated than conversational speech. This makes daily reading aloud a wonderfully language-enriching activity.

Strategies

As can be seen in the previous section, there are many language components present in books. There are many ways that we can incorporate these components into language targets. We need to consider the strategies that will supplement language learning. Below are some of the strategies that can be used to support language development while reading aloud.

Repetition

Repetition is a key way by which children learn new words. Children need to hear a word many times before they learn to say it. There is little consensus in the literature about the exact number of times a child needs to hear a word to learn to say it themselves, but we know that the more often they hear a word, the easier it is going to be to help them learn to use it. So we stress the importance of this strategy: repetition! Like any new skill, more exposure means it will be easier for us to master the skill.

As well as repeating new words, we can also repeat the book many times. This may not be a problem as children often request a book to be read again and again, seeming to take comfort from the familiarity of the story. While it can sometimes be tedious for the adult, it is reassuring to know that repeating the same story over and over is excellent for language development. Each time children hear the story repeated, they understand the concepts a little bit more and they grasp the sequence of the story with a little more certainty. Meghan Cox Gurdon tells us that 'children enjoy reading books because the experience imbues them with feelings of competency and mastery; because with each reading they understand a bit more of what they are seeing and hearing' (2019, p.102). In her book *The Enchanted Hour: The Miraculous Power of Reading Aloud in an Age of Distraction* (2019), she quotes a study from the University of Sussex where researchers explored the effects of re-reading. They concluded that there was a 'dramatic increase in children's ability to both recall and retain novel name-object associations encountered during shared storybook reading when they heard the same stories multiple times in succession' (Horst et al. 2011).

This is such a simple strategy to employ. Repeat words in the book and repeat the same books often.

Fewer questions

Quite often, we see parents, caregivers or educators asking children question after question, after question. These include questions such as 'What's this?', 'What's that?', 'You like apples, don't you?', 'What are you doing?' These are closed questions because they have a right or wrong answer. They typically require a limited response from the child – from a single word to as little as a head shake or nod. Questions can put children on the defensive and lead to them saying or doing less rather than more. Questions can stop the interaction, particularly if you are asking too many questions, asking questions that test the child's knowledge, questions that are too hard, questions that don't match the child's interests or questions that answer themselves (e.g. 'You like that, don't you?') (Stephan, 2016). While the adults can feel reassured when asking questions as this confirms their child's knowledge, for the child this barrage of questions just feels like a test, and the joy is taken out of the interaction. So how do we engage the child without bombarding them with questions? See the next strategy.

Commenting

Comments are far more helpful than questions for language development. What's even better is when there is a balance between questions and comments. Comments give the child the opportunity to hear words, phrases or sentences related to topics they are interested in. Essentially, children are learning a lot by simply hearing what you are commenting upon. We recommend that for every question you ask, you supplement the question with helpful comments to support the child in answering the question (Pepper & Wietzman, 2004). Learning language is not a test!

Talking about the picture

A similar strategy to commenting, talking about the picture exposes children to an array of alternative vocabulary that may not be in the text. In detailed illustrations, there may be more vocabulary in the pictures than in the text itself. Additionally, talking about the picture can sometimes bring the vocabulary in the text to life and help the child to understand the text and new words that arise. Some books have no text at all, and the story is told entirely through pictures. These 'wordless picture books' are great for language development as they force us to talk about the pictures and turn reading the book into a conversation.

Get face to face with the child

Getting face to face with the child is a staple strategy in the world of speech and language therapy and for good reason. First, it establishes a connection between parent and child which supports bonding and interaction. Second, being face to face offers the child the opportunity to see your face and mouth as you are talking. The child can see your face, with your facial expressions, gestures and how you form the words you are saying. This helps the child to focus on and take in what is being said to them. Being face to face also helps you follow the child's lead. You can do this by watching what they are interested in and responding to their interests contingently. This in turn gives you the opportunity to comment and add language to their interests, which is the best way to learn language.

Stress key words

Stressing key words means putting emphasis on important words you want the child to hear. For example, if you want a child to learn a new adjective, stressing that key word in the text draws their attention to that new word and helps them hear it. Stressing new words includes changing the tone of your voice, the volume and the animation.

Slow down

Slowing down the pace of reading is an effective strategy for many children. Like anyone, children and adults alike, learning new information can be supported by slowing down our rate of speech. This helps process new information. Children need more time than adults to process auditory information, and children with language delay or disorder need even more time. For example, for adults who have had the sensory experience of touching, tasting and enjoying the experience of eating watermelon, it is easy to quickly read over 'one slice of watermelon' in Eric Carle's *The Very Hungry Caterpillar* story without a second thought. For a 2-year-old, who has no life experience of this fruit perhaps, slowing down the pace and breaking up the syllables 'wa-ter-mel-on' can really help the child grasp this new word.

It is essential that we consider the speed at which we are reading. Although sometimes, out of pure exhaustion, parents just want to get through the book so the child will go to sleep, it is much better to read less, at a slower pace, to give the child an opportunity to process the story and follow the narrative. Jim Trelease, author of *The Read-Aloud Handbook* encourages us to 'read slowly enough for the child to build mental pictures of what s/he just heard you read. Slow down enough for the child to see the pictures in the book without feeling hurried' (Trelease & Giorgis, 2019, p.168). By reading slowly, we give the child a chance to process the language and visualise what is not shown in the picture. In her book *How to Raise a Reader*, Pamela Paul also recommends reading more slowly than feels natural to bring the rhythm of the text to life (Paul & Russo, 2019). Reading aloud more slowly forces us to read *with* the child, not *at* the child, and this supports the development of the child's language skills.

Waiting

A strategy that is closely linked to slowing down is 'waiting'. Waiting is a remarkably effective strategy for supporting language development. Waiting gives more time for children to process new information and more time to think of a response and work out how to express it.

Ways you can 'wait' include the following:

- When you turn to a new page in the book, say 'wow' and then wait up to 5-7 seconds before making any more comments. This gives your child the opportunity to take the lead and show you what they notice or are interested in on the page.
- If you ask a question about the book, wait to give the child time to process, think and respond. Wait up to 5-7 seconds.

If you are having a conversation about something in the pictures or the storyline of the book, wait. Give more time for the child to process, think and respond! Wait up to 5–7 seconds.

Pitch to child level

A surefire way to lose a child's interest in a story is if we pitch the language level too hard or too easy; both are equally detrimental to keeping the child engaged in the story. Remember when you were at a lecture in college? Irrespective of whether the lecture was too easy or too hard, your attention and interest waned. The same thing happens to children when they are not being challenged appropriately. If you are reading a book, it is quite easy to decrease the complexity to make it easier for the child or increase the complexity to make it more challenging:

Ways to simplify a story:

- Don't read the text, just talk about the pictures. Comment on what you notice.
- Shorten the sentences to make them simpler to understand.
- Explain difficult concepts or new and unfamiliar vocabulary.

Ways to increase the complexity of a story:

- Ask open-ended questions that encourage the child to think about the book in different ways and to problem-solve. Open-ended questions do not have a right or wrong answer, and they give the child an opportunity to think more deeply, solve a problem or make an inference. Open-ended questions really build and expand on the child's language and comprehension skills.
- Ask the child which character they like the best and why.
- Encourage the child to predict what might happen next.
- See if the child can relate the book to their own experiences.
- Compare and contrast different books on similar themes.

Dialogic reading

Dialogic reading is an interactive style of reading. It is a shared reading experience and it involves turning a book-reading interaction into a conversation whereby the adult and the child both play a role in the shared reading experience. There is much evidence on the efficacy of dialogic reading to improve vocabulary and language skills generally. Ramsey et al. (2021) investigated the effects of dialogic reading on the expressive vocabulary skills of children with moderate to severe expressive impairments. They found 'significant improvements' in expressive vocabulary after a four-week dialogic reading programme. A similar study by Simsek and Erdogan (2015) 'indicated that participation in the dialogic reading intervention had significantly changed children's receptive, expressive and total language scores'.

> Dialogic reading draws on sociocultural learning theory to suggest that scaffolded interactions between children and adults during reading will result in language gains, particularly with regard to vocabulary development, oral complexity and narrative skills. There is also evidence that the experience of dialogic reading correlates with future literacy skills.
>
> (Watkins, 2018)

Dialogic reading in the clinic

Dialogic reading in the clinic will most likely occur between a parent/caregiver and child or the speech and language therapist and the child. The speech and language therapist's role is to model dialogic reading but also to coach parents and caregivers through the dialogic reading experience.

Dialogic reading in the classroom

Dialogic reading in the classroom is best implemented between teacher and child or the teacher and a small group of children. Dialogic reading between the whole class can be challenging if all children wish to speak at the same time or make the same type of observations. Whole-class reading is best implemented coupled with open-ended questions whereby some children are selected to answer the questions. The role of the teacher in dialogic reading in a one-to-one context is to model language to the child, offer them opportunities to talk, take turns and have a fun conversation about each page.

Dialogic reading at home

Parents engage in dialogic reading by slowing down the read-aloud, talking about the picture and relating it to the child's own experiences. This type of reading is interactive and very child-centred with the parent following the child's lead in the conversation.

How to do dialogic reading

The basic dialogic reading technique uses the PEER acronym. This is where the parent/teacher:

P – Prompts the child to say something about the text
E – Evaluates the response
E – Expands on the child's answer by rephrasing it or by adding information
R – Repeats the prompts to see if the child has learned from the expansion

Explain the meaning of new words

Explaining the meaning of a word is a simple strategy that supports understanding of vocabulary. We cannot expect children to use new words in their own speech if they do not understand the meaning of the word in the context within which it was used. The level of explanation given will depend upon the child's age or language level.

How to explain a noun

Noun matrix:

CATEGORY	FUNCTION	PARTS
What group does new word belong to	What does it do? What is it used for?	What parts belong with this word
SENSES	**THE NEW WORD IS**	**PERSONAL EXPERIENCE**
Taste, smell, feels like	_____	Relate to a time That your child has experienced
WHERE DO YOU FIND IT	**LOOKS LIKE**	**ASSOCIATIONS**
e.g. kitchen, outside, Paris	Talk about shape, size, features	what goes with this? e.g toothpaste goes with toothbrush

Figure 3.1 Noun matrix

Example:

CATEGORY	FUNCTION	PARTS
Furniture	It's for sitting on	Has legs, arms, cushion, backrest
SENSES	**THE NEW WORD IS**	**PERSONAL EXPERENCE**
It feel soft	**Armchair**	You know the brown armchair in the sitting room that Dad loves?
WHERE DO YOU FIND IT e.g. in the sitting room living room, bedroom, hotels etc	**LOOKS LIKE** It's brown. Has a rectangular shape. It can be made of lots of different materials. It looks comfortable	**ASSOCIATIONS** what goes with this? e.g armchair and footstool armchair and sitting room, armchair and a coffee table

Figure 3.2 Example

Tool for describing adjectives

Use this tool to help provide in-depth teaching of adjective words.

Adjective matrix:

EXPLAIN THE WORD	**PUT IT NEW WORD IN A SENTENCE**	**ACT IT OUT/ DRAW IT** Act out or draw the meaning of the word!
COMPARE THE WORD TO SOMETHING THAT MEANS THE OPPOSITE	**THE NEW WORD IS:** _____	CHOOSE A WORD THAT MEANS THE SAME AS THE NEW WORD
PERSONAL EXPERIENCE Talk about a time when you experienced this word	ASSOCIATIONS; WHAT DOES THE NEW WORD REMIND YOU OF?	**PHON. AWARENESS** Clap out the parts to the word

Figure 3.3 Adjective matrix

Example:

Figure 3.4 Example

Use new words throughout the day

The use of the new word throughout the day. For example, if the new word was 'smooth', you could try to incorporate that word into experiences throughout the day. For example, 'Oh my teeth feel so smooth after brushing them', 'The mirror feels so smooth', 'Feel the apple, it's so smooth', 'This egg is so smooth too!'

Dedicating time to reading aloud daily

Have a dedicated time every day for storytime. Without this routine in place, books can easily be forgotten in a busy classroom. Remember that some children do not have the experience of hearing stories read aloud at home, so they may not have an appreciation for books and the joy within. These children may struggle in terms of attention and listening and may need support to sit and listen to a story. Dedicated time for reading aloud is particularly important for these children.

Relate new words to the child's everyday experience

Make sure to relate the new word to the child's everyday experiences (where possible). When a new word is incorporated into an appropriate context in the child's everyday life, it helps them gain a deeper understanding of what the word means. Model examples of how to use this new word in appropriate sentences throughout the day. Encourage them to use this word themselves throughout the day too. Parents, teachers and those central to the child are in the best position to do this.

To build comprehension of the story, make connections between the story in the book and personal life experiences. For example, you could be reading about Gerald the Giraffe who couldn't dance at the beginning of the story. You could relate this to the kids' own life by talking about how it was difficult to do the movements at the first gymnastics class. In this way, they can empathise with Gerald. Also relate the book to other books that you have read – for example, 'This reminds me of the story we read about the girl who couldn't draw, so she drew a dot.

Encourage visualisation as you read

Visualisation is a critical language comprehension technique and a skill that can be taught from the very beginning. Encourage children to visualise as you read. Pause frequently and talk to the children about the pictures you have in your head. Ask them if they have formed similar images. Visualisation is a key technique in language and learning. Visualisation allows us to combine left- and right-brain functions. Cue the child by saying, 'I see...' or 'That makes me think...' Include detailed descriptions which reflect the descriptions in the text incorporating colour, shape and size adjectives. Encourage the children to make a 'mind movie' and tell you back what they are 'seeing'.

Encourage prediction

Before you begin a new book, introduce the book to the children by taking a good look at the cover and having a 'cover conversation'. Encourage the children to make predictions regarding the story and what clues the front cover gives. Draw the children's attention to the author and whether they are familiar with him/her. Draw their attention to the illustrator and the style of illustration. You can also encourage the child to predict during the read-aloud by talking about what might happen next and why they think that.

How to read a wordless picture book

There is no right way to read a wordless picture book. Here are some of our top tips for reading wordless picture books:

- Talk about the cover of the book, what do you notice? What clues are there on the front cover to let you know what the book is about? What does the title tell us? Ask open questions to encourage the child to think about what the book is going to be about. 'I wonder…' questions are a nice place to start. This is a great way to develop the skills of predicting and problem solving.
- Talk about what you notice on each page. Because there is little or no text, the author has to be certain that they make their meaning clear with the pictures.
- Once you become familiar with the book, you could add in some book language such as 'Once upon a time…'
- Ask the child open questions about the book such as:
  - What did you like about the story?
  - Who was your favourite character and why?
  - What is your favourite illustration and why?
  - How do you think they feel and why? Did you ever feel like the main character?
  - Who showed bravery/courage/fear/humour?
- Encourage the child to tell you the story in their own words. If your child is reluctant, prompt gently with questions such as who, what, where, when, why.
- Repeat the book many times if your child enjoys it. As you become more familiar with the story, add in voices for different characters and sound effects or change your tone of voice as the story requires.

Cover questions

Before you even open a new book, a nice way to develop language skills is to have a 'cover conversation'. This prepares the child for the story and piques their interest in storytime. It is an opportunity to give the child some background knowledge about the topic and it also encourages higher-level language skills such as problem solving and predicting.

- I wonder what this story is about.
- How do you think the boy feels? Why?

- The title of the book is *One Frog Too Many*. What clues does that give us?
- I see two frogs. What do you think is happening?

Sharing a book with a child can be both enjoyable and beneficial to a child's language development. These simple yet effective strategies can go a long way in helping to expand a child's language skills such as vocabulary, grammar, sentence structure and inferencing basic concepts, among many more. In this chapter, we have detailed how to read a book to get the most out of it for language development. With these simple strategies, we can turn reading a picture book into a wonderfully language-enriching experience.

4 Phonological awareness and strategies

What is phonological awareness?

Phonological awareness is the ability to notice the sound structures of a spoken word. It is the awareness that sentences are made up of words, words are made up of syllables, and syllables are made up of individual sounds. Children need to have strong foundations in phonological awareness before learning to read and write.

Several critical reviews of the efficacy of phonological awareness intervention have provided concrete evidence that phonological awareness can be improved through instruction and intervention. Also, improvement in phonological awareness leads to improvement in word decoding (Ehri et al., 2001; Bus & Van IJzendoorn, 1999; Schuele & Boudreau, 2008). Studies show that phonological awareness difficulties are indicative of later reading difficulties or dyslexia. Difficulties with phonological working memory have also been observed. We must first consider the foundational levels of awareness and question whether phonological awareness tasks that require deeper levels of awareness and understanding are gradually introduced.

For example, rhyming is a foundational skill in learning to read. This is why it is important that children are exposed to rhyme, listening to rhyme and generating rhymes themselves, before more complex literacy skills. Rhyming is a precursor to the more complex phonological skill set. Rhyming sets children up to tune in and listen to the parts of a spoken word. It helps to hone in and discriminate between sounds and words that sound the same and those that sound different.

To work on phonological awareness successfully, it's important to understand how phonological awareness develops so that we know to sequence tasks that range from easy to more difficult. Phonological awareness skill progresses in a predictable pattern. All the elements of phonological awareness develop as part of a complex continuum. One skill does not necessarily develop before another but ultimately, like the reading rope skill set, each of the individual skills supports the others.

DOI: 10.4324/9781003262961-4

Continuum of Phonological and Phonemic Skill Complexity		
less complex ⟶	COMPLEXITY	⟶ more complex
WORD AWARENESS	SYLLABLE AWARENESS	PHONEME AWARENESS
		Isolation What is the first/last/middle sound in *fan*?
Sentence Segmentation How many words do you hear in this sentence?		**Identification** Which word has the same first sound as *car*?
		Categorization Which word does not belong? *bus, boll, house*?
Blending Listen as I say two small words: *rain .... bow*. Put the two words together to make a bigger word.	**Blending** Put these word parts together to make a whole word: *rock....et*.	**Blending** I'm going to say a word slowly. What word am I saying b - i - g?
Segmentation Clap the word parts in *rainbow*. How many times did you clap?	**Segmentation** Clap the word parts in *rocket*.	**Segmentation** How many sounds in *big*? Say the sounds in *big*.
Deletion Say *rainbow*. Now say *rainbow* without the *bow*.	**Deletion** Say *pepper*. Now say *pepper* without the *er*.	**Deletion** Say *spark*. Now say *spark* without the *s*.
		Addition Say *park*. Now add s to the beginning of *park*.
		Substitution The word is *mug*. Change *m* to *r*. What is the new word?

Figure 4.1 An adapted version of Rachel Woldmo's Phonological Awareness Table of Complexity

What is the role of the speech and language therapist (SLT) in supporting phonological awareness in young children?

1 Our first step is to develop our own knowledge about phonological awareness, including its important link to literacy success. We must recognise, at a professional level, the important role that SLTs play in the area of pre-literacy skill development as it has an important role in speech clarity and speech sound development.

2 We need to raise awareness of the importance of phonological awareness within our profession and educate and boost colleagues' knowledge to ensure phonological awareness is consistently considered within the speech and language assessment and treatment process. Attention should be given to the implications of phonological awareness not only on literacy development but also on language and intelligibility skills.

3 SLTs can provide the most effective and reliable assessment of phonological awareness in children. This includes screening and/or in-depth assessment. Tests that assess phonological awareness include the Phonological Awareness Test (PAT) and the Clinical Evaluation of Language Fundamentals 4 (CELF 4).

4 SLTs may provide phonological awareness intervention to the children on their caseloads, either embedded within other language goals or as an explicit intervention target. SLTs may also be most suited to provide phonological awareness intervention in small groups (in schools or otherwise).

5 SLTs may consult or collaborate with classroom teachers on phonological awareness instruction and/or intervention for children on their caseload as well as for children within the general education curriculum. SLTs can collaborate with classroom teachers to enhance phonological awareness instruction within the general curriculum. They can identify phonological awareness skills that are developmentally appropriate and developmentally sequenced (Wanzek et al., 2000).

6 SLTs also can assist teachers in providing differentiated classroom instruction that better meets children's varying learning needs. Alternatively, SLTs can collaborate with the special education teacher or literacy teacher who can provide or lead on the intervention.

What is the teacher's role?

1 Teachers play an essential role in supporting phonological awareness in the classroom setting as it underpins and provides a basis for all future literacy. It is essential to provide children with the basics so that all children are starting out on a level playing field as early as possible. It is a mistake for primary teachers to rush into teaching phonics without establishing a clear baseline of strong phonological awareness skills.

2 Teachers should incorporate phonological awareness activities through-out the day in the classroom, both at preschool and primary school levels. As well as reading aloud to support phonological awareness, teachers can develop phonological awareness throughout the day by highlighting rhyming words, segmenting multisyllabic words and breaking down sentences as they come up.

3 The teacher should flag those children with phonological awareness difficulties and differentiate the work provided to those children. Teachers can identify children struggling with phonological awareness by implementing a phonological awareness screening tool, such as the screening tool in Appendix 1.

4 Teachers should liaise with parents and provide them with information about the importance of phonological awareness for supporting reading and writing skills.

5 The phonological awareness skills focused on in this section include:
   - Rhyming
   - Blending
   - Segmentation
   - Deletion
   - Isolation
   - Substitution

Rhyme

Step 1: Exposure to rhyme

Sing songs, recite nursery rhymes and read nursery rhyme books and rhyming stories to expose children to plenty of rhyme. Rhyme is a critical component of early sound awareness.

- Sing or recite nursery rhymes daily.
- Read rhyming books and highlight rhyming words as they arise (e.g. you could say: 'Each Peach Pear Plum, I spy Tom Thumb. "Plum" and "Thumb"- those words rhyme'). Popular rhyming books include:
  - *Peepo* by Janet and Allen Ahlberg
  - *Each Peach Pear Plum* by Janet and Allen Ahlberg
  - *Giraffes Can't Dance* by Giles Andreae and Guy Parker-Rees
  - *Brown Bear, Brown Bear, What Do You See?* by Eric Carle and Bill Martin Jnr
  - *The Gruffalo* and other Julia Donaldson books
  - *There's a Bear on My Chair* by Ross Collins
  - *The Pout-Pout Fish* by Deborah Diesen and Dan Hanna
  - *Rosie Revere, Engineer* by Andrea Beaty and David Roberts

  o *The Caboose Who Got Loose* by Bill Peet
  o *The One with the Waggly Tail* by Sarah Webb and Steve McCarthy (poetry collection)
  o *For Laughing Out Louder* (poetry collection)
  o *Where the Sidewalk Ends* (poetry collection)
  o *Mother Goose's Nursery Rhymes* by Axel Scheffler
- Rhyme Bingo: Pick a picture and match the picture with each picture on a bingo board. Express your thoughts as you go (e.g. you say, '"Ball", "table" – no, they don't rhyme. "Ball", "watch" – no, they don't rhyme. "Ball", "fall" – yes, they rhyme.').

Step 2: Identifying rhyme

Identify rhymes during read-alouds.

- During read-aloud sessions of rhyming stories, nursery rhymes or songs, you can check in with a child to see if they can identify rhymes.
- Play a game where you make deliberate mistakes in familiar nursery rhymes or rhyming stories and encourage students to spot the mistake (e.g. 'Incy Wincy spider climbed up the water spout, down came the rain and washed the spider away').
- After read-aloud time, play 'Odd one out': Read aloud a list of three or four words and have them identify the ones that rhyme and the odd one out that does not rhyme (e.g. 'dog, log, cat, fog' or 'cot, lot, book, rot').
- Before children line up, ask each child if two words rhyme (e.g. 'Do these words rhyme? "Lot, key". Do these words rhyme? "Lo, tot".'). You may need to practise this as a whole group initially.
- Put pairs of rhyming pictures in a 'feely' bag. Children take turns pulling out two cards. If the two cards rhyme, they keep the pair. If the cards are different, they are placed back in the bag and the next person has a turn. The winner is the person with the most pairs of rhyming words at the end.
- When taking the roll call, have each child decide if two words rhyme after their name is called.
- Rhyme Bingo: Pick up a picture and move it along all the pictures in the first row of the bingo board. As you go, label the pictures (e.g. '"Wall, tree" – do they rhyme?'). Give the child the opportunity to say 'yes' or 'no' to each pair of pictures. Repeat with each row of the bingo board.

Step 3: Generating rhyme

Encourage children to generate their own rhymes to finish off an alternative ending to the sentence.

- Choose five words from a science/geography/history lesson and have the class think of words that rhyme with each one.
- Have students think of words that rhyme with numbers during a maths lesson (e.g. one/fun, two/shoe, three/bee).
- Play or sing nursery rhymes or rhyming pop songs (for older children). Leave out the last word in a line and see if they can guess the missing word based on the rhyming word from the last line (e.g. 'Hickory dickory dock, the mouse ran up the...').
- Rhyme 'I spy': Play 'I spy' but give a rhyming clue instead of a letter cue (e.g. 'I spy with my little eye, something that rhymes with sore').
- Write a swap poem. You write one line of a poem and have the student write the next line, matching the rhythm and rhyming the last word. (Hint: Use words that are easy to rhyme!) This activity could also be carried out with students in pairs, with the teacher supporting them as needed.
- Create rhyming word families on the (interactive) whiteboard. Write up a word ending (e.g. -ab) and have children choose a letter to add at the beginning to create rhyming words (e.g. cab, lab, tab). Nonsense rhyming words can be discussed if/when they arise (e.g. 'Nibble, dribble - those words rhyme and they are real words. What about wibble?').
- Silly picnic game: Collect some food together - either real or play food - and put it in a bag. Make up silly nonsense rhyming clues to see if students can guess what you are taking on the pretend picnic. Saying lots of silly nonsense rhyming words gives them the chance to hear the rhyme lots of times and this will help them to guess (e.g. 'Felly welly, telly, will we take a wobbly...(jelly)?' or 'Liskets, fiskets, miskets, I want to take a packet of...(biscuits)').

Blending during read-alouds (suitable for 5+)

- When you come across compound words in a read-aloud, use the opportunity to break the word up into the word parts. For example, if the word is 'snowman', show the child that the word is made up of two smaller words.

Blending activities

- Blending compound words: Give pairs of children a picture of a compound word such as 'rainbow'. Put out pictures of the words making up the compound words - rain and bow -and get the children to find the smaller words that make up their compound word.
- Use a 'robot' voice to say multisyllabic words with a pause between each syllable. Children have to blend the syllables and say the word. To make it easier, choose a particular theme (e.g. children's names, months of the year, foods).

You can extend it and choose harder categories as the child gets better (e.g. countries or dinosaurs!).

- Choose one word during a lesson and say it sound by sound, to see if the students know what word you are saying (e.g. 'Colour the circle r...e...d').
- You could use blocks to represent each phoneme and then push them together when the children say the word. This would be a helpful visual cue for some children.
- Divide the class into groups and give each person in the group a card with one sound on it (e.g. 'f', 'sh', 'i', etc.). Ask them to make words by combining their sounds.
- Call out attendance by saying the students' names one sound at a time (e.g. "Is f-i-l here?" Name: Phil).
- Before going to another part of the school (library, hall, office, etc.), say the name of the place one sound at a time and ask the students where the 'mystery place' is.
- Guessing game (similar to robot Robbie Robot game except at sound level): Ask children to guess which things in the classroom you are saying in a funny way (e.g. b-a-g, b-oo-k, ch-ai-r). Start with shorter words (2-3 phonemes) and progress to longer words. You could work through words from different categories/topics.

Segmentation during read-alouds

- Break up sentences; ask children to count how many words they hear in a short sentence (3-5). Clap out the words. When books are repeated, children almost know them like a mnemonic: 'A mouse took a stroll through the deep dark wood.' This then gives the opportunity to develop awareness of sentences and the word boundaries within, not to mention the morphological and syntactic structure therein.

Segmentation activities

- Tap out the syllables - break up longer words. Again, read-aloud time is the ideal way to introduce multisyllabic words in a fun and enjoyable way. Teachers can model segmenting the word into its constituent parts and children can be given the opportunity to try. The benefit of hearing a story repeated throughout the week means that the child will have repeated opportunities to hear these longer words and how they are segmented.
- Have the class clap out the syllables in each child's name during attendance.
- Clap out the syllables in spelling words for the week.
- Clap out the syllables in words on the word wall.

- Clap out the syllables in new vocabulary words as you learn them.
- Clap out the syllables in the names of the days of the week, months of the year, etc. (e.g. 'To-day is Mon-day Jan-u-ar-y fif-teenth').
- Counting your fingers: The teacher says a word. The children use their fingers to count the syllables in words. They hold up one finger for each syllable. Let the fingers display until counting is completed.
- A body place for each syllable: Touch your head for one syllable, head and shoulders for two, head, shoulders, hips for three, head, shoulders, hips, knees for four, etc. Use interesting words (e.g. children's names).
- Duck duck goose: Tap one child on the back for each syllable. Say the whole word to one child and then they are 'on'.

Deletion during read-alouds (suitable for 5+)

- During book sharing, when a child has a multisyllable name, ask the class to take away one syllable and tell you what's left (e.g. 'Rainbow. What's rainbow without the rain?'). Begin by deleting initial syllables as this will be less challenging than final syllables.

Deletion activities

- At the start of the day at attendance call, when a child has a multisyllable name, ask the class to take away one syllable and tell you what's left (e.g. 'Jennifer. What's Jennifer without the "fer"?'). Begin by deleting initial syllables. This will be easier than final syllables.
- Have each child delete a syllable from a word before lining up for yard.
- Have the students delete one syllable from each spelling word for the week, then add it back in (e.g. 'Our spelling word is "gravity". Can you say gravity without the first part "gra"?').
- During a lesson, have the students 'clap out' the syllables in a new vocabulary word. Then ask them to take away one of the syllables (e.g. 'In-su-late. Say insulate without the "in".')
- Have the students take turns picking an object in the room with two or more syllables. Then ask each one to say their word without one syllable. (e.g. Alison picks the computer, so you ask her to 'say it again, but don't say "ter".').

Isolation during read-alouds (suitable for 5+)

- Guess the sound: When you are reading aloud a story, choose some words in the story that have the same sound in the word. Tell your students you want them to guess which sound is the same in a group of words you say to them (e.g. bed, book, blue). The students will repeat the words and then determine the sound in common.

Isolation activities

- Guess the sound: Tell your students you want them to guess which sound is the same in a group of words you say to them (e.g. carrot, kitten, caramel). The students will repeat the words and then determine the sound in common.
- Match the sound: This activity requires students to listen to several familiar words in order to determine which sounds are similar within the words. This activity can be easily done with student names. For example, choose two or three students in the class whose names start with the same sound (George, Julia, Jane). Ask the students what the matching sound is in the name. Be sure to point out matching sounds and not matching letters! Each day, name a group of different students and ask them what the matching sound is. For an added challenge, ask students to think of one more word starting with that same sound.
- Train visual: The concept of beginning and end sounds in words may be challenging for many children at this level. They may benefit from having a visual representation of the beginning, middle and end of a word. For example, this could be done with an image of a train where the train's driver carriage, middle carriage and end carriage can represent the beginning, middle and end sounds of a word, respectively. Start with words with three phonemes (sounds) such as dog, cat, hat, man or sun, and avoid consonant clusters such as in glove and hand. Vowels are much harder for young students to hear, so many children will have difficulty listening for the middle sound.
- Listening for sounds: Ask the children to listen for particular target sounds as you read familiar lists of words, sentences, poems, songs or stories to them. Their job is to raise their hand each time they hear the target sound. It may be helpful to model or demonstrate this task to familiarise the students with the task before starting. Sounds at the start of words will be easier than sounds at the end or middle of words, and consonants will be easier for children to detect than vowel sounds.

Substitution during read-aloud (suitable for 5+)

- Substitute a phoneme for the title of well-known books (e.g. 'the Bruffalo' (*The Gruffalo*) or 'Mear Moo' (*Dear Zoo*)).
- Substitute a phoneme for all the initial sounds of a popular rhyme (e.g. Mary had a little lamb – 'Mary mad ma mittle mamb').

Substitution activities

- Get children to turn to the person beside them and swap the initial sounds of their names (e.g. 'Katie and Maria' would be 'Matie and Karia').

Note

Adapted from the phonological awareness working group with the Demonstration Project on In-school and Early Years Therapy Support, 2019.

Some of these activities were adapted from Rachel Woldmo's leaflet 'Phonological Awareness: An Instructional and Practical Guide for Use in the Kindergarten Classroom'. Available here: www.uwo.ca/fhs/lwm/teaching/dld_2018_19/ Woldmo_PAGuideKindergarten.pdf

5 How to choose a good book for language development

The choice is endless when it comes to choosing children's picture books. With thousands of new children's books published every year, choosing the best books for language development may seem like a daunting task. We have made a list of our favourite books for language development which can be found in Chapter 8. If you are choosing a book to use in the clinic room or the classroom, here are some things to consider. Some children's books promote vocabulary learning better than others, and choosing the right kind of book to support language development is important. Parents might be drawn to books that their child is interested in or one that might even reflect a TV show that the child enjoys watching. While reading any kind of a book is better than not reading any book at all, there are children's picture books out there that are of 'better quality' for supporting speech and language skills. We have put together a matrix to make the selection process easier.

Tick three or more and you probably have a great children's book!

Good range of words and interesting vocabulary	Detailed illustrations	Interactive/ sensory books
Story has rhyme and rhythm	Story promotes empathy/ inclusion/ diversity	Engaging/ fun/ interesting story
Story has lots of repetition	You enjoy reading this book	Book matches your child's interests/ seasonal topics

Figure 5.1 How to select a good children's book

DOI: 10.4324/9781003262961-5

1. Detailed illustrations

For language development, it is important that we choose books that have detailed illustrations as they tend to be more of a talking point. They draw us in and encourage us to pay attention to the story for longer and to comment on what we see. This exposes children to even more vocabulary and promotes dialogic reading. Children's book illustrators are not always given the credit they deserve for the critical role they play in the creation of a picture book. The illustrations bring the story to life for the child. Many children are visual learners, and their understanding of the language within the story is supported through quality illustrations. Illustrations often offer clues to what might happen next, and this encourages the child to infer and predict. The colours that an illustrator chooses set the mood and tell us more about the characters and their emotional state. This helps to clarify the meaning of the text and gives the child a greater understanding of the language of the story. Detailed illustrations support your child's understanding of the book. It gives them visual cues to help them piece together the elements of the story. Illustrations allow adults to incorporate more sophisticated vocabulary as they can describe the picture, adding more vocabulary to the interaction based on what is happening in the pictures. The child in turn also has the opportunity to ask questions about the pictures, promoting a back-and-forth discussion.

2. Books that you enjoy

If you don't enjoy what you're reading, you may unintentionally give that impression to the child, and this will not help to get or keep the child's interest in the story. For example, think about the expressions or the change in the tone of our voices while reading a book we love compared with a book we don't. I realise that I cannot hide when I like or dislike a book, or anything else for that matter! If I don't like a book, I find myself rushing through it, speaking faster (Irish people do tend to speak rather quickly!). The tone in my voice is flatter, and I'm simply not captured by the book, so I fail to capture those around me. It's truly so obvious and stark! Think back to your childhood and recall those teachers you loved! I bet it's easy to explain why you liked them; they were most likely engaging, fun, helpful, dynamic, interested in you and your classmates. Children know when we're not actually 'engaged' or 'interested' in working with them – they're wiser than we give them credit for! As the saying by Maya Angelo goes, 'People will forget what you said, people will forget what you did, but people will never forget how you made them feel'. Children are far more likely to engage and enjoy a book if you are enjoying the book too. Choose books that you enjoy reading as this will help make reading aloud more of a habit and less of a chore. If you are reading aloud a story that you don't enjoy, it will be difficult to put any positive emotion into it, as it just feels like a hardship. The child will sense this and the pleasurable interaction is reduced to a speedy read to get it over as quickly as possible. I have no shame in saying that I have hidden *Thomas the Tank Engine* books, never to see the light of day again!

3. Books that interest the child

This one is obvious but has to be mentioned. Sometimes we read and share books with children with our own goal or 'agenda' in mind. Sometimes that can't be helped! However, bear in mind the level of interest the child has in these instances. If they don't appear engaged or appear to be losing their marbles from sheer boredom, it's probably best to change tack! Children will stay attentive to a book they enjoy and like, so finding the balance between a book you both enjoy is the ideal.

4. A good range of interesting words and vocabulary

There are books out there with high-quality and low-quality language content. After viewing and analysing many picture books, we found that books with more computer-generated illustrations were less likely to have a good array of vocabulary within the pictures. Furthermore, we also found that books based on TV programmes did not have the type of vocabulary that is important or useful in language development.

5. Books with rhyme

Rhyme supports phonological awareness skills. Phonological awareness is an important pre-literacy skill. So books that include lots of rhythm and rhyme are excellent for supporting this critical pre-literacy skill. Julia Donaldson's books are our top choice for rhythm and rhyme. Books with rhyme help children become more aware of sounds and how to discriminate between sounds. Children with good rhyme awareness have a greater understanding of language and how words are formed.

Culturally, nursery rhymes are very much a part of childhood and still play a really important role. The ability to fill in the last word in a rhyme or to copy part of a nursery rhyme hones the child's listening skills. Nursery rhymes expose children to new vocabulary and introduce new concepts. Children who present with delayed language skills often struggle to recite a nursery rhyme. While some nursery rhymes may be a little outdated, there are plenty more besides. Check out Chapter 8 for some of our favourite nursery rhyme books.

6. Books that support learning about emotions, inclusion and diversity

Stories that promote empathy, inclusion and diversity help the child to learn the vocabulary in these areas. Books can really support the child to learn the language of emotions, and this gives the child the tools to express their own emotions as they come up. Books also help children understand about others who are different, and they promote acceptance, tolerance and patience. There is a growing availability of books that help children understand autism, Down syndrome, hearing impairment, dyslexia and anxiety, as well as differences in race, colour and culture. This is a great resource for teachers who may have a child in their class who presents with some differences. This will help the children learn the language and understand the needs of this child.

7. Stories with lots of repetition

Children learn by repeatedly hearing, seeing and doing. This applies to every aspect of development. Therefore, the more children hear words, the more opportunity they have to learn them. Books that repeat words are great for developing language, particularly in younger children. Alternatively, by re-reading good-quality books often with your child, you are exposing them to all the rich language in the text or embedded in the pictures. Re-reading is fantastic for developing language, and the chances are that every time you read the book to your child, they will pick up something new! The principle for learning vocabulary is similar to that of learning to ride a bicycle. The more exposure and the more practice the child has, the more easily the skill can be mastered. Choosing books with repetition promotes vocabulary learning as repetition is how we learn language. Stories with repetitive text can be simple stories such as *Brown Bear, Brown Bear, What Do You See*, where there is something new added on each page. But they can also be more complex stories such as Julia Donaldson's *What the Ladybird Heard*. Both of these books have a repetitive storyline that is almost like a mnemonic for the child's language system, helping them to learn the language in a fun, rhythmic, repetitive way.

8. Sensory/interactive books

Books that are interactive are great for young children. This includes books that have flaps, buttons, pop-up pictures or different types of materials incorporated into the illustration. Sensory books are a feast for the senses! These types of books are also great for children who really need sensory input! For example, many children with autism have sensory needs and enjoy different types of sensory input to help regulate themselves. Interactive stories with different textures also contribute to language learning. The *That's Not My* range by Fiona Watt and Rachel Wells is a great example. There are touchy-feely patches on each page and this helps the child learn the new word. For example, 'That's not my fairy, her hairy is too *fuzzy*'. Lift-the-flap books are a great way to keep a child engaged for longer. Choose the cardboard version of these books as they are much more durable, and look out for the lift-the-flap books that have felt flaps which are easy for younger children to manipulate. The Usborne non-fiction books also have excellent lift-the-flap features that young children love.

9. Seasonal or topical books

Choosing books that relate to a holiday or an event that is imminent in your child's life is naturally going to get their attention as it relates to them and their interests. Non-fiction books could also be included here as certain topics may be of particular interest in your child's life. This could be a good strategy to try with children who are reluctant readers! Choosing seasonal books has an obvious impact on vocabulary development as it helps the child learn the words that correspond to that time of year, be it spring, Halloween or Christmas. Rotate books and bring out seasonal books at the appropriate time. This helps to keep the child interested and there are always new books to enjoy. The library is a great resource for seasonal books, but be sure to get there early so you have the book in time.

10. Engaging, fun, interesting stories

Laughter and fun are important components of learning. Choosing books that are fun will also promote vocabulary learning. When children are engaged in a fun read-aloud that makes them laugh, they are learning language without any struggle. As they watch the woodpecker peck more and more holes into things in Lucy Cousins' book *Peck, Peck, Peck*, they are hearing words such as 'aubergine', tangerine' and 'sardine', and as they giggle, they are oblivious to the learning that is happening! There are so many fun books to choose from, and these books will help to engage even the most reluctant child. Some of our favourite fun books include *My Friend Bear* by Jez Alborough, *The Wonky Donkey* by Craig Smith and Katz Cowley, and *Don't Let the Pigeon Stay Up Late* by Mo Willems.

6 Picture books in education settings

The development of oral language skills is an essential component in classrooms everywhere. Language development underpins all other learning, so it is a crucial aspect of any curriculum. In Ireland, for example, one of the main themes of the Aistear Early Childhood Curriculum (National Council for Curriculum and Assessment, 2009) is 'Communicating'. Communicating is about 'children sharing their experiences, thoughts, ideas, and feelings with others with growing confidence and competence in a variety of ways and for a variety of purposes' (Centre for Early Childhood Development & Education, 2006). Books are identified as a key resource for developing this theme. The aim is that an educator 'ensures young children experience a print-rich environment and fosters their love of excitement in, understanding of, and use of books' (Centre for Early Childhood Development & Education, 2006). They recommend that exposure to books begins with babies and continues as the child grows and develops. Similarly in Britain, the Early Years Foundation Stage (Department for Education, 2014) identifies communication and language development as a key area of learning. Oral language is the basis for all learning. Without it, an in-depth understanding of a particular subject would be extremely challenging. Reading picture books aloud can supplement so many other areas of the child's development – for example, imagination and creativity, numerical concepts, culture, nature, empathy, social and emotional development, appreciation of different art forms and styles, appreciation of opinions and different perspectives. The Oral Language Strand of the Irish Primary Language Curriculum (National Council for Curriculum and Assessment 2019) identifies 12 units which are concerned with the development of language. The support material highlights the importance of picture books as a resource for development of this strand.

Teachers can support language skills development during read-alouds in either small or large groups. Small groups are more supportive for children who present with language difficulties or other developmental delays, and it would be wise to peer-match their abilities and communication styles so that the children are all given an equal opportunity. Quite often in a group context, a chatty and social child can dominate the teacher's time and attention as they are most likely to interact,

DOI: 10.4324/9781003262961-6

initiate interactions and answer questions. Speech and language therapists and teachers must become aware of those children who interact but do not necessarily participate in read-aloud time. They can support children who are struggling with their language by using the language strategies in this chapter.

The Hanen Centre (www.hanen.org) has trained facilitators who roll out the Teacher Talk programme. Teacher Talk is an excellent programme for early years educators on encouraging language development in the preschool setting. Part of this programme helps teachers become aware of the child's conversational style and the type of role they play as an educator while interacting with the children.

Environmental considerations

Setting the scene for a reading-aloud experience cannot be underestimated. Today's fast-paced world filled with screens and distractions often overshadows more present and calm activities such as reading aloud. Reading aloud requires sustained attention for extended periods, and if there's one thing we know from everyday experience, it is that the draw of technology in today's society is constantly pulling us from the present moment. By setting up a book nook in our homes and classrooms, we invite children into the present moment to share a story in a comfortable space without interruptions.

Book area

A book nook is a small quiet area in your house/classroom dedicated to reading and sharing books. Therapists can work with parents and advise them on how to set up a book nook in their home so that books become part of family life. A book nook could also be set up in a clinical waiting area, giving parents another opportunity to share a story with their child as they wait for their appointment. Similar ideas can be tried out in the classroom. How you set up the environment for reading aloud really makes a difference. Try out some of the tips below to get the most out of read-aloud time. A book nook should be a cosy, relaxed and fun space. It should be decorated in a way that invites your child over to read. We want children to be in an environment where they are not reading books because it's something they were told to do. We want children to read books because the subliminal message sent to the child in their home/classroom is that books are toys and that they are there to be enjoyed!

Create a book nook

The four factors to think about when creating a book nook are:

1 **Comfort:** Decorate the space in a way that your child will like – for example, a blanket, lamp, beanbag or comfy chair. Fairy lights are always a novelty addition,

but this will depend upon your child's style. If you and your family are into essential oils, you could also use some oils that promote calming to match the space.

2 **Quiet:** Choosing a quiet space is best. This means it is best to try to find or create a space where distractions are limited. So make sure no phones are within reach and TV/music is switched off.

3 **Light:** It's hard to read where there is little light and it's tricky to read with too much light (e.g. reading with the sun in your eyes). So getting the lighting right is important to set the right mood and atmosphere for reading.

4 **Book display and book storage:** Consider how you store the books. Book covers are designed by illustrators specifically for children. They are designed to attract children's attention. Storing some books facing outwards will entice the child over to read them. Quite often, books are stacked on shelves and only the spine of the book can be seen. This must be very disheartening for illustrators who spent so much time and energy trying to create covers that will grab children's attention!

In summary, think about your reading-aloud space: just a few little tweaks could make all the difference to the reading experience.

> Reading should not be presented as a chore or a duty but presented as a precious gift.
>
> Kate DiCamillo

How to read a book to support language development

There is an art to sharing a book with a child that helps to gain their attention, engagement and interaction. Once we have the child's attention and engagement, this forms the basis for subsequent language development. Here are some ideas on how to share a book in the school setting to get the most out of it for language development.

Before reading the book

•   Read the book yourself and familiarise yourself with the text so that you can read aloud in a fluent manner, knowing where to pause, inflect or change your voice. Complete a cheat sheet (Appendix 3) on the book to help analyse the content. Consider the vocabulary and concepts in the book. Is there a way to help the children connect this book to their everyday life experiences? Consider whether you might need to provide the children with some background knowledge before reading the book to help them understand the storyline.

•   Introduce the book title and author. For example: '*The Very Hungry Caterpillar* by Eric Carle.'

- Have a 'cover conversation'. Talk about the front cover and help draw their attention towards the book. Encourage the child to make predictions about what the book may be about and what clues are provided on the cover.

While reading the book

- Read the text, slowly turn the page.
- Stress novel words.
- Repeat the novel words and point to the picture.
- On repeated readings, wait expectantly for the child(ren) to take a turn.
- Talk about the picture, pitching it to the child's level.
- Relate to personal experiences where appropriate.
- Ask open questions where appropriate.

After reading the book

- Discuss the book, talking about the storyline/characters. Be sure not to bombard the children with too many content questions and thereby turning the discussion into a test. Try to make it a discussion. Talk about favourite parts and why. Model for the child by expressing your own opinions and preferences.
- Manage the discussion so that all children have the opportunity to speak. Discuss the importance of turn-taking in the group. Think about how children who have developmental differences could be incorporated into the discussion. Equally, there should be no pressure on a child to comment if they do not wish to contribute.
- Consider an extension activity. Compare and contrast to similar books. Read a related non-fiction book to help develop the child's background knowledge on the topic. Model acting out the story during pretend play.

How to create a language-rich classroom

1. Read a picture book every week

We feel that a book of the week is a great way by which teachers can incorporate reading aloud into the daily classroom schedule. A picture book can help meet the language requirements of the preschool Aistear Early Childhood Curriculum (2009). It can also meet the requirement of every element in the Oral Language Strand of the Primary Language Curriculum (2019) – see Appendix 4. By reading the book once a day, the children become familiar with the vocabulary, and as the week progresses, they really have a great sense of the book. It is in the latter part of the week that the children's language can be challenged more with open questions, and we can encourage them to make connections with personal experiences. Use the cheat sheet in Appendix 3 to help select language targets for the week and consider how the book will link to other strands in the curriculum. See also Appendix 5 which shows how the themes of Fallon's Rainbow Oral Language Programme are linked to appropriate picture books.

While the child's reader will challenge them in terms of decoding the text, often these early readers lack the richness of vocabulary that a quality picture book will have. Furthermore, the sentences in these early readers are, by their very nature, simplistic in terms of their syntactical and grammatical structures. Some children may arrive at school without having heard stories read aloud to them. By reading aloud picture books, you give all children an opportunity to hear rich language structures and vocabulary

2. Selecting appropriate vocabulary targets

It's important to think about the types of words that are useful. The best words are those that build upon conceptual understanding, can be used in a lot of different contexts or have alternative meanings

What are the most helpful types of words to teach children?

Words that are useful, that build upon conceptual understanding, can be used in a lot of different contexts or have a lot of uses (Elklan, Language Builders Elklan .co.uk). These words are 'high-frequency' words in that they come up in different contexts or situations often. They can sometimes be more common in writing than in everyday speech. Some high-frequency words that come up often are 'several', 'attention', 'obvious', 'natural'.

For example, when selecting useful words, choose vocabulary that comes up a lot in everyday experiences in the classroom such as 'several', 'divide', ''separate, 'equal'. Also think about words you do not think children fully understand in stories that are read aloud (e.g. humorous, ravenous, exaggerate).

Below are some questions to think about when trying to select appropriate vocabulary.

- **How useful is the word?**
  - Does the word appear often in written text?
  - Does the word appear frequently across the school day and come up in more than one subject?
  - Is this a word that does not often come up in everyday conversation?
  - **Examples:** 'categorise' and 'technique', range broadly in use

- **Does the word build on conceptual understanding?**
  - o Does the word describe a concept that the students already know in a more precise, specific or sophisticated way?
  - o **Examples:** 'ravenous' for 'hungry', 'hindrance' for 'something that is getting in the way', 'cooperate' for 'working together'.
- **Can the word be used in a variety of contexts?**
  - o Is the word used in at least more than one context?
  - o Does the word have several uses?
  - o **Examples:** 'dull' can mean 'blunt', 'not very bright' or 'boring'; 'set' can be a noun (e.g. 'a movie set', 'a set of china dishes') or a verb (e.g. 'she set her mind to it', 'please set the table') (Talktime, 2019).

3. Generalising language throughout the day

The most important way that teachers can help with the generalisation of new language and vocabulary is to model the targets. Incorporate new vocabulary from picture books into the classroom conversation, as children learn by hearing new words used in context. In a language-rich classroom, teachers are talking a lot and modelling how language is used. It is this deliberate and repetitive use of new vocabulary in a meaningful way that makes the real difference. Help the children engage with the new vocabulary with meaningful conversations about the book and the theme generally. The art of conversation can easily be lost in today's modern world where technology dominates.

Other ideas for generalisation of new vocabulary include:

- Extension activities
- Reviewing words
- Visual word walls

Extension activities

Extension activities help to bring stories to life for children. They help the child gain a better understanding of elements of the story and also provide an opportunity to reinforce new vocabulary and language-learning goals. Extension activities help children connect the book to real life and they also give children a chance to use language in a new way. Extension activities are a fun way to delve deeper into the story.

Ideas for extension activities

1 Bringing the story to life through pretend play can be a really simple and fun way to extend a child's learning and help them remember language from the

book. With the use of simple props, children can play around with the story. Use story sacks and puppets to bring the story to life. For example, a caterpillar toy munching away at some food gives the child the opportunity to use the language in this story again and again, 'but he was still hungry'. For older children, we can encourage them to act out the story with different children taking different parts. In *Room on the Broom* by Julia Donaldson and Axel Scheffler, kids love to take on the different character roles and say their lines: 'I am a frog as clean as can be. Is there room on the broom for a frog like me?' In this way, children have the opportunity to practise new vocabulary, grammar and sentence structure in a fun way.

2   Sing songs related to the story.
3   Art and craft activities: colouring, drawing, painting, play dough.
4   Building background knowledge and linking to non-fiction books to build vocabulary around that topic. You can build background knowledge about a certain topic in other ways, such as watching a YouTube video based on the topic, going on a nature walk if the topic is related to nature, or completing a simple science experiment to help the comprehension of the material and language. Matching the story with a similar book or with a non-fiction book. This is a great way to help children build background knowledge on a topic. For example:

Fiction	Non-fiction
Rosie Revere, Engineer by Andrea Beaty and David Roberts	*How Things Work* (Usborne)
What the Ladybird Heard by Julia Donaldson and Axel Scheffler	*The Great Irish Farm Book* by Darragh McCullough
The Smeds and the Smoos by Julia Donaldson and Axel Scheffler	*Look Inside Space* (Usborne)
The Little Red Hen by Paul Galdone	*Chickenology* by Barbara Sandri, Francesco Giubbilini and Camilla Pintonato
The Tiger Who Came to Tea by Judith Kerr	*Life-Size Animals: An illustrated Safari* by Rita Mabel Schiavo and Isabella Grott
The Lorax by Dr Seuss	*Old Enough to Save the Planet* by Loll Kirby and Adelina Lirius
The Very Hungry Caterpillar by Eric Carle	*The Big Book of Bugs* by Yuval Zommer

Alternatively, pair up two fiction books with similar themes to compare and contrast and generate lots of language and discussion. Examples include:

o   *Owl Babies* by Martin Waddell and Patrick Benson and *The Owl Who Was Afraid of the Dark* by Jill Tomlinson
o   *An Evening at Alfies'* by Shirley Hughes and *All Afloat on Noah's Boat* by Tony Mitton and Guy Parker-Rees

5   Going on a field trip that relates to the story. For example, after reading about animals, you might take a trip to the local pet farm or zoo. If the story is based in woodland, you might go for a walk in the local forest.

6   Watching the movie of the story where available or watching a related screen-time documentary.

4. Make books central to the classroom

Build up a classroom library consisting of high-quality picture books. One good-quality picture book can target multiple language areas, so be mindful about what books you invest in.

- Create a welcoming book nook in your classroom. Also display books in other areas of the classroom so children think of them as a 'toy' to be explored as opposed to something that is kept just for storytime.
- Do a review of your book area. Discard any books that do not meet standards (see Appendix 2). Discard books that are shabby and torn.
- Do regular book rotations to keep the children's interest. Try to include seasonal books where possible. The library is a great resource for seasonal books but be sure to order books early so you have them in time.

5. Educate parents

Empower parents to build oral language skills at home. Educate parents on the important role oral language has on later reading and writing skills. Inform parents of the book of the week, perhaps give them a summary of the storyline and encourage them to talk about the book at home with their child.

Many primary schools have school libraries. In this case, consider giving a picture book for homework once a week. The expectation is that the child will listen to their parents reading a story and enjoy the luxury of this quality time spent together. This helps parents create the habit of reading aloud regularly. Support parents to engage in dialogic reading by showing them how to read a book for language development. Encourage parents to continue reading aloud to their children even as they progress through school and become proficient readers themselves. Generally, adults can read at a higher level, so we can always expand their language skills. Local libraries also provide library cards for preschools and schools.

7 Picture books in the speech and language therapy clinic

Role of the speech and language therapist

The overarching goal of picture book use in speech and language therapy treatment plans is to incorporate naturalistic communication and language strategies into an interactive read-aloud experience for babies, toddlers and young children. As books are typically woven into the fabric of their early life, they are (hopefully) already within the child's everyday context and experience; if it's not already woven into their everyday experience, that's where you need to start with parents/caregivers. The research strongly details the benefits of reading aloud on language development and much more, so it makes perfect sense to utilise books for language learning.

How to use picture books in the clinical setting

Step 1: Assess

Your role as the speech and language therapist (SLT) will be to first assess the child's language skills. This can be done either informally or formally. It would especially be important to have a good understanding of their expressive language skills.

Step 2: Set goals for child and parent

Based on your findings, the next step will be to set goals appropriate for this child. Parents should always be involved in the process of setting goals. Goals must also be set for the parent.

Please see the suggested goals below for both the child and the parent.

Step 3: Choose appropriate books

Refer to Chapter 8 for how to choose appropriate books. Use the cheat sheet in Appendix 3 to analyse the book for appropriate language targets.

DOI: 10.4324/9781003262961-7

Step 4: Educating

Coaching includes educating parents about language development and in particular reading aloud. Coaching relates to educating parents about why pictures should be included in a child's everyday life. It includes educating parents about how to get the most out of books to support speech and language development by incorporating many different types of strategies.

Step 5: Modelling

Modelling strategies during the read-aloud.

Step 6: Coaching

Parents can be coached during the session. Alternatively, a video from home can be a very useful tool for increasing awareness about how to incorporate strategies during read-alouds.

Our top tips for SLTs

Display picture books in your clinic room

While there are benefits to working with a child in a clinical setting, the research suggests that children learn best in their own environment. I work in a clinical setting where we provide assessment and intervention to parents and children 'on our turf' so to speak. From my many years' experience working in this kind of setting, I have come to realise that clinical settings may not always be conducive to supporting children and their families to their best potential. Sometimes I find that clinic rooms can be 'sterile' environments and lack the warmth or comfort that prepares minds and bodies for learning. However, we can try to make our clinic rooms as inviting as possible, and by displaying books in our clinic room, we can model what we expect from parents. Have some picture books displayed, along the window sill or on a low table. You will find as a therapist you will reach for these books more and more if they are readily available.

Despite the challenges of a clinical setting, there is much that we can do. Clinical settings allow us to train and coach parents about how to support their child's language at home. In the clinical setting, we can model how to read books to support language development. How we 'set the stage' for enticing children is very important.

Educate and coach parents

When I introduce the idea of the importance of picture books for supporting language in therapy sessions, there is always one tip I recommend to parents. I encourage them to be mindful of their home environment. I help them to reflect on how much emphasis they place on books and reading aloud at home – to think about whether books are visible and easily accessible to the child, whether the books are stacked uninvitingly on a shelf, out of reach or difficult to see, whether a child is giving ample opportunities to see and watch parents read themselves or read aloud to the child. As the saying goes, 'Monkey see, monkey do'! If children are exposed to an environment that emphasises the importance of books, they will be more inclined to have a positive regard for books and reading. If a child's first experiences with books begin in primary school learning how to read, this may result in a negative regard for books as they perceive books as 'work', 'hard' or 'unenjoyable'. Having reviewed many picture books for the purposes of writing this resource book, it's clear that authors and illustrators know what they are doing. See leaflets for parents in Appendix 6.

Familiarise yourself with some of the recommended picture books

Get to know the content so you can learn how to use these books for language development. When considering goals for therapy, think to yourself, 'Do I have a book that targets this?' A book is always more fun than a worksheet. A few good-quality books will be plenty to support many language goals for children of varying ages. You as a therapist can go to the library and borrow books for clinical use.

Encourage parents of your clients to bring in the child's favourite book into every session

More often than not, you can incorporate the book into a pre-existing goal that has been set for the child.

Organise a local book drive

By organising a book drive locally, you as a therapist will have access to a library of books to give to families who are in your service. Check out the resources from www .bookfairypantryproject.org. In our experience, people are often delighted to donate books to a worthy cause.

Local charity shops often have surplus children's books that they are willing to give away. Local libraries will sometimes donate books that are going out of circulation. We found that the books donated from the library service are of high quality so this is worth pursuing.

Local schools are usually willing to facilitate a book drive also. A local school in our area recently organised a book swap where every child was asked to bring a book to donate. They could then choose a new book for themselves. Of course, there were surplus books and they kindly donated them to the speech and language therapy department.

Also allocate some department funds to order some good-quality books that can be used as a clinic resource. Check out our lists of recommended books in Chapter 8.

Give parents information about the library services

Have library service application forms printed off to give out or have website details ready.

Link with your local health nurse

Public health nurses (PHN) are the first link most families have with the health service for their child. Educate PHNs about the importance of reading aloud to children from the very beginning. See leaflets in Appendix 6.

Link with families in your area

Organise training with parents on the importance of reading aloud. Consider using your local community resource centre. These are great community hubs and are accessible and familiar locations for local parents. Consider vulnerable/minority groups in your area who may need extra support and who may find our service difficult to access. Also consider hosting a presentation event for the families in your service about how to use books to get the most out of language. Give our resources in Appendix 2 and 6 to parents to train them in how to select the best kind of books for supporting engagement, language development and pre-literacy skills. Use our tool in Appendix 7 to help develop vocabulary of nouns and adjectives that come up in books.

Functional targets for picture books

We have included a bank of goals to help with setting goals for clients in the clinic. There are goals for attention and listening, interaction and engagement, language comprehension, expressive language, higher-level language skills and phonological awareness during the read-aloud.

Attention and listening

- The child will attend to one book for increasing lengths of time.

Interaction and engagement

- The child will initiate a request for a story to be read aloud through non-verbal or verbal means with 80% success.

- The child will participate by interacting with the sensory elements of the picture book with 80% accuracy (lift-the-flap, touchy-feely books, noisy books).
- The child will demonstrate evidence of joint attention by looking at the communication partner and back at the book with 80% success.
- The child will reference the communication partner with non-verbal communication with 80% success (eye contact, looking, gestures facial expressions).
- The child will communicate with the communication partner for the purpose of:
  o getting attention
  o requesting
  o commenting
  o keep the story going
  o protesting.
- The child will imitate actions, gestures, sounds and words with 80% accuracy.
- The child will take turns with the communication partner with 80% success (turning a page, filling in a word, filling in an action).

Language comprehension

- The child will point to familiar items in the book upon command with 80% accuracy.
- The child will show comprehension of early concepts, where appropriate, with 80% accuracy.
- The child will show comprehension of early verbs as they appear in the read-aloud with 80% accuracy.
- The child will show comprehension of less familiar verbs with 80% success.
- The child will show comprehension of prepositions with 80% accuracy (on, in, under, between, beside, over, etc.).
- The child will show comprehension of adjectives with 80% success.
- The child will show comprehension of who, what, where, when questions about the book with 80% success.
- The child can identify character traits and emotions and relate them to personal everyday experiences with 80% success.

Expressive language

- The child will imitate sounds appropriately with 80% success.
- The child will imitate words appropriately with 80% success.
- The child will spontaneously make sounds appropriately with 80% success.
- The child will spontaneously label objects appropriately with 80% success.
- The child will spontaneously label actions appropriately with 80% success.
- The child will complete the ending of a familiar sentence or rhyme (words or phrases) with 80% success.

- The child will use a word, phrase or sentence to describe the picture with 80% success.
- The child will answer 'wh' questions appropriately with 80% success.
- The child uses sequencing vocabulary appropriately to retell part or all of the story (e.g. first, next, after that, last, etc.).
- The child can retell part of all of the story with 80% success.
- The child will define new words with 80% accuracy.

Phonological awareness

- The child can finish a rhyme with the appropriate rhyming word at the end of the sentence with 80% accuracy.
- The child will identify words that rhyme when given a choice between two words with 80% accuracy.
- The child will generate their own rhyming word with 80% accuracy.
- The child will segment syllables in words of increasing length and complexity with 80% accuracy (e.g. caterpillar, fox, Gruffalo).
- The child will segment sentences into words with 80% accuracy.

Higher-level language

- The child can make predictions and inferences about the storyline with 80% success.
- The child can compare and contrast objects, settings and illustrations with 80% accuracy.
- The child can compare and contrast characteristics or emotions in characters.
- The child can compare and contrast 'the main idea' between two books.
- The child can identify idiomatic language in books with 80% accuracy.
- The child can predict an alternative ending to the story with 80% success.
- The child will define new words in depth with 80% accuracy.

Suggested targets for the communication partner (CP)

- The CP will build knowledge and awareness around language development and the importance of picture books for supporting language development and also literacy skills.
- The CP will repeat target vocabulary often during the read-aloud without affecting the flow of the shared reading experience.
- The CP will follow the child's lead in the selection of books by giving them a choice.
- The CP will reduce their closed questions and turn those questions into comments by 70%. Alternatively, comment four times for every question you ask.

- The CP will slow down and talk about the pictures, where feasible and appropriate.
- The CP will wait for the child to initiate a comment during a familiar story.
- The CP will wait for the child to respond to a question by pausing and waiting expectantly.
- The CP will pitch the language to the child's level during the read-aloud experience.

These goals can be used across different contexts such as in the clinic room, as part of a home programme or as identified goals for a teacher or preschool teacher with whom you are liaising. Once you have a target selected, the next step would be to select the best kind of book to target this goal. Have a look in our book recommendation section below for selecting the best kind of book to target a goal above. Alternatively, check out Appendix 2 which has a tool to help you select the best kind of book.

Special considerations

Reading aloud has benefits for all children, but for some children with different developmental challenges, it can have specific benefits. There are, however, things to consider when reading aloud to children with developmental differences and here we will look at this in a little more detail.

Reading aloud to autistic children

Books are a great way to bond with children, and for autistic children, books may be a great way to build and develop their interaction skills. Every autistic child presents in a different way, and while we recognise this, we can offer some general advice for reading aloud to this cohort.

Some autistic children will have no interest in books. If this is the case, don't worry: their interests may change over time. For these children, I would have books in their environment and take out a book frequently but not pressurise them to sit and listen to a story.

Think about the child's sensory profile. If the child likes deep pressure, encourage parents to snuggle them up in a nice cosy blanket for story time. Autistic children and adults can be sensitive to light, sound, taste, smells. A great tip for keeping them engaged for as long as possible is to find a comfortable space that has limited external sounds and smells. In the school setting, reading a book in a library room or calming space away from the hustle and bustle of a classroom might help the child engage best.

Sometimes fidget toys are helpful if you find that they need to move their hands to regulate themselves.

For autistic children, it's particularly helpful to choose a book that you know they have an interest in. This is an important step to getting your child interested and engaged in a reading routine. You must follow your child's lead and read books of their interest.

Following their lead is important when choosing a book that you think they will like, but it's also important for you to try to follow their lead as you read the book together. Let your child lead the way! So if your child wants to hear the text on the page, by all means read it. If your child wants to only look at the pictures, that's OK too. In this instance, comment on what they are looking at on the page or comment about what is happening on this page. Let the pictures guide you if your child wants to only look at the pictures.

Sometimes your child may not want to hear the story being read; other times they want you to read the test verbatim. The most important thing is that he/she is enjoying the special bonding time reading with you.

Autistic children have unique learning styles. They can quite often be very visual learners. This is why books that have lots of detailed illustrations can help keep them interested and engaged, and also help them understand the story.

Autistic children also can often have specific interests. These could include transport items or animals or space. You could think about reading different types of fiction books to them but also look out for non-fiction books about their interests. This is a great way to learn and also encourages reading books for enjoyment!

Some autistic children can have difficulties understanding hidden meanings and 'turn of phrases' in books. So taking the time to use simple language to explain what is happening on the page while using the pictures to help them will support their understanding. Books offer the opportunity for inferencing, theory of mind and empathy in a unique kind of way. There is more information on this in Chapter 2.

Reading aloud to children with developmental language disorder (DLD) or other learning difficulties

The importance of reading aloud to children who have DLD or learning difficulties cannot be overstated. Reading aloud can bolster their learning in so many ways, and the best part is that it can be fun and enjoyable!

Repetition helps learning. Many kids have to overlearn in order to integrate new information. Read-aloud stories offer a unique opportunity for this kind of repetition in a fun engaging way. Children love to hear their favourite stories again and again. For example, if a child is struggling to learn new concepts in language such as 'under' and 'in', teaching them these concepts in books is more fun, compared with drilling them in table-top activities in the clinic room or classroom! We often use the book *Dear Zoo* in the clinic room to teach concepts such as 'big', 'tall' and 'grumpy'. Children love to complete the sentence 'He was too...BIG, so I sent him...BACK'. Of course, you can still do drill-type work if you feel the child needs it, but by using books to teach concepts, the child has an opportunity to learn in a different way that may be more fun and appealing to them. We all know that the more engaged a child is, the better the child learns!

Sometimes it can be hard to come up with new ways to teach concepts a child is struggling with. If we are honest with ourselves, as speech and language therapists we are sick to death of teaching concepts using the same old worksheets or with the same old activities and games!

This is why reading aloud is so good for teaching concepts. Reading aloud is beneficial for all aspects of language. There is an array of books with brilliant illustrations just waiting to be used to support language development. Prepositional concepts – 'under', 'on', 'in', 'between', etc. – are present in a multitude of illustrated children's books. You simply have to extract that language from the pictures and show parents how to do the same. Similarly, concepts such as 'before/after' and 'first/last' are evident in every book! Other concepts like 'big/small', 'empty/full' and 'wet/dry' are commonly seen in children's books too.

Reading aloud with a child supports their attention page by page, book by book, as they sit and delight in stories. Some children can attend better if they are given the space to fidget and move their feet to get the sensory feedback they need in order to regulate themselves enough to stay focused on the story. Research shows that reading aloud has a huge impact on brain development. This is true for all children, but it is definitely an important consideration for children who have DLD or learning difficulties.

Reading aloud also helps your child to understand so much about books – learning how to turn the pages, learning how sentences flow across the page from left to right and the concept of 'the end'. Furthermore, your child learns about words, how they are made up and how to break them down, and they learn about rhyming. These are known as phonological awareness skills, and they are the very early skills that a child learns when beginning to read. So reading aloud to your child who has difficulties with learning is especially important because it sets them up for learning how to read themselves.

Reading aloud to bilingual children

Picture books can be a great resource for bilingual language learners. Picture books can help maintain a mother tongue when the child's language environment is dominated by their second language. Mary-Pat O'Malley is a speech and language therapy researcher and lecturer at the National University of Ireland Galway. She is passionate about multilingualism. In a recent interview with her, she talked about how bilingual or multilingual children need adequate skills in all languages to participate fully in all aspects of their life. She believes that books are a great tool to support the maintenance of their home language as the home language can be particularly vulnerable in an environment that is dominated by a second language.

A 2020 article in the journal *Child Development* examined bilingual language learners in Norway who received a book-based language intervention programme (Grøver et al., 2020). The study included 464 children aged 3–5 years, who were acquiring Norwegian as their second language in preschool and spoke a variety of first languages at home. They received a researcher-developed intervention that was organised around loosely scripted, content-rich shared reading in school and at home. Receiving the intervention had significant impacts on the children's second-language skills. Not only did the programme benefit the children's vocabulary and grammatical development, but benefits were also observed in the children's emotional states, resulting in a greater ability to see things from another person's point of view. Whether it's supporting a non-dominant language or supporting the acquisition of a second language, picture books are an excellent resource for bilingual and multilingual children.

How can we support bilingualism through the use of picture books?

- Encourage parents to read aloud in the home language.
- If parents don't have books in their home language, encourage them to share the book by talking about the pictures. This type of dialogic reading is great for language development. Books are an ideal way to expose a child to a second language including more abstract language, which may not come up in daily conversation.
- Parents can also read wordless picture books – books whose story is told entirely through pictures. This means they can be 'read' in any language. Picture books can also help children connect with their diverse cultures, helping them maintain links and have an understanding of their unique backgrounds.

Reading aloud to children with dyslexia

The building blocks for reading begin well before the first day of school. As detailed in Scarborough's reading rope (see Chapter 2), many of the skills required for successful reading actually begin before the first day of school. The foundations of reading include attention, comprehension, expressive language and phonological awareness. Therefore, it is essential to consider a child's pre-literacy skills in order to determine if any underlying deficits are contributing to a diagnosis of dyslexia.

Because reading can be a real struggle for some people with dyslexia, they may come to dislike books and have an aversion to reading. This may, in turn, impact academic performance. Children who have had early experiences with the joy of picture books may develop a more positive relationship with books and reading. This readies them for the challenges of academic books and more complex reading structures. If a child's first experience with reading is based on decoding skills, they may have a very different outlook on books compared with a child who has been read to since the day they were born.

An interesting study led by Heikki Lyytinen (2015) highlights that dyslexia is not something that turns 'on'. It is not something that is non-existent before a child learns to read. The researchers in this study assessed 200 children, half of whom were at risk for dyslexia, from birth to puberty on hundreds of measures. They did neuro-recordings from the infant's scalps to track neural responses to Finnish speech syllables. When they followed the child through subsequent years, they were able to find that the neural signal was predicting vocabulary development at age 4, and reading development in later years as well. We know how critical vocabulary knowledge is for the development of fluent literacy skills. There is strong evidence to show that people with dyslexia have trouble with vocabulary knowledge. Reading aloud from a young age is one of the best ways to enhance vocabulary development, and this in turn will support children who may be at risk of dyslexia.

Reading aloud picture books can have great benefits for children with developmental delays and disorders as well as those with neurodivergent presentations. It is a simple thing to do that has exponential benefits for the child.

8 Book recommendations

0-2 years

1. *Faces* by Baby Focus: First Touch

This book is for brand-new babies to help develop their eyesight. It includes a variety of high-contrast black, white and yellow faces. There is also a mirror at the end so baby can look and smile at their own reflection.
   Great for:

- Vocabulary development: face and facial features
- Getting familiar with books

2. *Mother Goose's Nursery Rhyme Book* by Axel Scheffler

This delightful collection of nursery rhymes is illustrated by the extremely talented Axel Scheffler. His illustrations have great success in keeping children engaged and getting the conversation flowing. This book is suitable for children aged 0-5 years.
   Best for:

- Rhyming text
- Vocabulary development: nouns, verbs, adjectives, concepts
- All phonological awareness

3. *Where's Spot?* by Eric Hill

Where's Spot? is a much-loved classic. This book is a great book for developing understanding of prepositions in a fun and interactive way; the lift-the-flap feature is sure to keep children engaged.

DOI: 10.4324/9781003262961-8

Best for:

- 'Where' questions
- Prepositions

4. *First 100 Board Book Box Set* (three books) by Roger Priddy

A simple yet effective book. Ideal for exposure to basic vocabulary targets. Brightly illustrated with images of real objects rather than cartoons! Photograph and written word underneath every image. Ideal for children aged 0–2 years.

Best for:

- Vocabulary: first 100 words
- Vocabulary: animals
- Vocabulary: colours and shapes

5. *That's Not My…* book series by Fiona Watt and Rachel Wells

This gorgeous book series is aimed at very young children. Brilliant bright pictures are sure to gain their attention. The patches of different textures support sensory development. The repetitive language in this book is ideal for new talkers!

Best for:

- Adjectives
- Repetitive text
- 'Not' concept
- Interactive, textured features

6. *Peepo!* by Janet and Allan Ahlberg

This book is simply magical. There is so much detail in these illustrations, offering plenty of opportunity for language development. Children aged 0–4 years can benefit from the wide range of vocabulary in this book. The rhyming text is great for supporting phonological awareness. The interactive features and the predictable, repetitive storyline in this book keep toddlers engaged.

Best for:

- Rhyming text
- Repetitive text
- Vocabulary: home, family

7. *Dear Zoo* by Rod Campbell

This book is appropriate for children aged 1–3 years. Its bright colours and lift-the-flap features help gain and keep attention and engagement. The repetitive storyline and array of concepts are great for toddlers! Check out other books by Rod Campbell such as *Dear Santa*, *It's Mine* and *Oh Dear*.

Best for:

- Repetitive storyline
- Concepts
- Vocabulary: early animals

8. *Each Peach Pear Plum* by Janet and Allan Ahlberg

This enchanting book is filled with many nursery rhyme references. The illustrations in this book are visually rich and detailed. Children will love spotting all the hidden details in the pictures and be sure to get a conversation going about everything happening in this book.

Best for:

- Dialogic reading
- Rhyming text
- Repetitive text
- Vocabulary: house, countryside

9. *Ten Little Fingers and Ten Little Toes* by Mem Fox and Helen Oxenbury

There are few things sweeter than tiny baby fingers and toys. This book is simply charming, and you will love reading it as much as sharing it with your little one. This book is filled with gorgeous illustrations. The rhyming, repetitive text primes young developing brains with the foundations for learning to read. The sense of belonging as you shift through the pages celebrates babies of different ethnicities and cultures from around the world.

Best for:

- Rhyming text
- Repetitive text
- Cultural diversity

10. *Tickle* by Leslie Patricelli

This brightly coloured book is a fun way to engage little ones. Nice simple illustrations and a great way to talk about body parts.

Best for:

- Vocabulary: body parts

2-3 years

1. *Postman Bear* by Julia Donaldson and Axel Scheffler

This charming book is part of the Acorn Wood series and it has beautiful illustrations, interactive lift-the-flaps and a nice strong structure which supports narrative development. Check out the other books in the series also such as *Fox's Socks*, *Rabbit's Nap* and *Hide-and-Seek Pig*.
   Best for:

- Rhyme
- Vocabulary: woodland animals, birthday party
- Early 'wh' questions: 'who', 'what'

2. *Mr. Brown Can Moo! Can You?* by Dr. Seuss

This classic book is full of silly sounds, rhythm and rhyme. It has lots of repetition and is great fun to read aloud.
   Best for:

- Rhyme
- Sound awareness

3. *The Very Hungry Caterpillar* by Eric Carle

Another classic book which was first published in 1969. This book has bright, bold illustrations and tells the story of a little caterpillar who eats his way through the book before pupating and turning into a butterfly.
   Best for:

- Vocabulary: food
- Multisyllabic words: caterpillar, strawberry, watermelon, lollipop, butterfly, sausage

4. *Monkey Puzzle* by Julia Donaldson and Axel Scheffler

This clever book tells the story of a little monkey who is searching for his mum in the jungle, helped along by a kind butterfly. Suitable for children 0-5 years.
   Best for:

- Vocabulary: jungle animals, adjectives
- Concepts: negation

- Rhyme
- Multisyllabic words: monkey, parrot, spider, butterfly, elephant, crocodile, caterpillar

5. *We're Going on a Bear Hunt* by Michael Rosen and Helen Oxenbury

This much-loved book tells the tale of a family adventure. Beautiful illustrations and an engaging, repetitive storyline. Suitable for children aged 1–5 years.
Best for:

- Wordplay
- Dialogic reading
- Targeting 'b' sound

6. *Goodnight Digger* by Michelle Robinson and Nick East

Beautifully illustrated book with repetitive text which is perfect for the bedtime routine.
Best for:

- Vocabulary: vehicles
- Rhyme

7. *Peck, Peck, Peck* by Lucy Cousins

This is a fabulous, fun, heart-warming book with bright, bold illustrations and interactive holes for little fingers to wiggle through. Suitable for children up to 5 years.
Best for:

- Vocabulary: home, food, clothes
- Rhyme
- Multisyllabic words. aubergine, tangerine, magazine
- Targeting 'p' sound

8. *Terrific Trains* by Tony Mitton and Ant Parker

This book is full of rhythmic rhyme and detailed illustrations. The book brings non-fiction to life with information about trains presented in a fun and engaging way. Check out other books in this series including *Tremendous Tractors*, *Dazzling Diggers* and *Super Submarines* for all those vehicle-crazy preschoolers. Suitable for children up to 5 years.

Best for:

- Vocabulary: vehicles
- Excellent range of adjectives and verbs
- Rhyme
- Targeting 't' sound

9. *Good Dog Carl* by Alexandra Day

This is a fun wordless picture which tells the unusual story of Carl, a Rottweiler who takes care of the baby while mom is out.

Best for:

- Vocabulary: home
- Dialogic reading

10. *Cars, Trucks and Other Things That Go* by Richard Scarry

This is a fun and somewhat outlandish book with detailed magical illustrations on the topic of vehicles. So much to talk about and notice on each page. Perfect for dialogic reading.

Best for:

- Vocabulary: vehicles, adjectives
- Dialogic reading
- Open questions: 'I wonder…'

11. *Giraffes Can't Dance* by Giles Andreae and Guy Parker-Rees

This is a charming book about a giraffe who struggles to dance like the other animals but in the end finds his own rhythm. Suitable for children up to 5 years.

Best for:

- Vocabulary: jungle animals, dance
- Development of empathy for someone who is different
- Overcoming adversity
- Rhyme and rhythm

12. *Owl Babies* by Martin Waddell and Patrick Benson

This is a story of three baby owls who are nervously waiting for their mother's return. It's a delightfully reassuring story which supports the child who has separation anxiety.

Best for:

* Dialogic reading
* Structured narrative

13. *Pip and Posy: The Super Scooter* by Axel Scheffler

Pip and Posy are two friends who often face a little challenge in their day. In this book, Posy snatches Pip's scooter, but then falls and hurts her knee. There is a whole series of *Pip and Posy* books, and we love them for their simple text and detailed illustrations.

Best for:

* Dialogic reading
* Simple narrative for early sequencing and narrative skills
* Vocabulary development
* Targeting 'p' sound

3-5 years

1. *The Kissing Hand* by Audrey Penn, Ruth E. Harper and Nancy M. Leak

This is a classic story which is read widely to children to help them prepare for school and the anxieties that often come from separating from loved ones at this time.

Best for:

* Emotional preparedness for school
* Developing vocabulary on the topic of separation

2. *One Frog Too Many* by Mariana Mayer and Mercer Mayer

This wordless picture book tells about the adventures of a little boy and his pets. It explores emotions such as jealousy, sadness, guilt and happiness.

Best for:

* Dialogic reading
* Open questions
* Emotional vocabulary

3. *The Gruffalo* by Julia Donaldson and Axel Scheffler

This tale of a clever little mouse who tricks the animals in the wood is world-famous at this stage. It is a fun and engaging story, and it's also great for language development.

Best for:

- Rhyming text
- Multisyllabic words: laughter, crumble, Gruffalo, underground, terrible, scariest, everyone
- Vocabulary: woodland vocabulary
- Targeting 'm' sound

4. *Pig the Pug* by Aaron Blabey

This is a hilarious story of a greedy dog who won't share his toys.

Best for:

- Rhyming text
- Empathy: emotions such as greed and kindness, as well as the theme of sharing
- Targeting 'p' sound
- Open questions: 'I wonder…'

5. *Marvin Gets Mad* by Joseph Theobald

Marvin the Sheep explodes with anger when his friend takes his apple. This funny story explores themes of anger and temper tantrums.

Best for:

- Emotional vocabulary and empathy
- Vocabulary
- Targeting 'm' sound

6. *Alfie…* book series by Shirley Hughes

The Alfie book series is a beautifully told set of stories with tales of the simple day-to-day events in Alfie's family. The illustrations are detailed and nostalgic, and cause the reader to look just a little longer. The books explore a variety of themes such as kindness, jealousy, fear, joy and friendship.

Best for:

- Vocabulary: family and school life, adjectives, verbs
- Narrative
- Development of 'wh' questions
- Open questions
- Dialogic reading

7. *Hairy Maclary from Donaldson's Dairy* by Lynley Dodd

This book tells the tale of Hairy Maclary who goes for a walk with some of his friends and what happens when they meet Scarface Claw, the toughest cat around.
  Best for:

- Short simple narrative
- Sequencing
- Rhyming text

5+ years

Picture books

1. *The Lion's Share* by Matthew McElligott

This terrific book tells the tale of a tiny ant who receives an invitation to dine with the lion along with other guests from the jungle. She is shocked by the behaviour of the animals and wants to make it up to the king by baking him a cake. Lots of fun ensues when the other boastful guests turn it into a competition. Unique illustrations.
  Best for:

- Vocabulary development: jungle animals, excellent range of verbs, adverbs and adjectives
- Concept development: half, twice, middle, quarter
- Open questions and dialogic reading

2. *The Squirrels Who Squabbled* by Rachel Bright and Jim Field

This is a fun story of two greedy squirrels who find themselves in a race for the last pinecone of the season.
  Best for:

- Vocabulary: nature vocabulary, a rich variety of verbs, adverbs and adjectives
- Great for phonological awareness with rhyming text and multisyllabic words
- Explores themes of sharing, greed and having to work together in the end
- Targets the 's' sound

3. *The Lorax* by Dr. Seuss.

The Lorax is the original eco-warrior and, like all Dr. Seuss books, this is a fun story with lots of wordplay.

Best for:

- Rhythmic rhyming text
- Sound awareness

4. *On a Magical Do-Nothing Day* by Beatrice Alemagna

This is a story of a child who feels bored and just wants to play video games all day. When the video game falls into a pond, all seems lost until the world around seems to come alive.

Best for:

- Descriptive vocabulary
- Stunning illustrations which foster dialogic reading
- Open questions and narrative development

5. *The Lighthouse Keeper's Lunch* by Ronda and David Armitage

This modern classic tells the story of Mr Grinling the lighthouse keeper and his wife who must think of a way to stop the greedy seagulls from stealing the lunch she prepares for him every day.

Best for:

- Vocabulary: food vocabulary, maritime vocabulary
- Narrative development

6. *The Smeds and the Smoos* by Julia Donaldson and Axel Scheffler

This extra-terrestrial story of friendship highlights the importance of diversity and inclusion. No matter what our cultural differences are, they should not separate us. The rhyming text, the vocabulary, the wordplay and the illustrations are just phenomenal.

- Vocabulary development
- Wordplay
- Rhyming text
- inferencing

7. *The Snail and the Whale* by Julia Donaldson and Axel Scheffler

This beautifully illustrated book tells the tale of a snail who goes on an adventure on the tail of a whale. This book sends a powerful message of confidence despite size. The rhyming text is superbly orchestrated and coupled with rich vocabulary and detailed illustrations – a winning combination for supporting vocabulary development. Appropriate for children aged 3–6 years.

- Sophisticated vocabulary: verbs, adjectives
- Rhyming text
- Inferencing

8. *The Wonky Donkey* by Craig Smith and Katz Cowley

The Wonky Donkey is a hilarious book about a donkey. The rhythm, rhyme and repetitive text keep the attention of children of all ages. There is a surprising higher-level language component, which is great for interpreting and inferring the meaning of words and phrases. For different reasons, this book is appropriate for children from ages 2–6 years.

- Rhyming text
- Repetition
- Inferencing
- Sophisticated vocabulary

9. *Rosie Revere, Engineer* by Andrea Beaty and David Roberts

This clever, witty book is a delight to read. The book motivates children to have courage and follow their passions and interests. The creative storyline is filled with fantastic vocabulary, rhyming text and multisyllabic words. This book is great for children aged 4–8 years.

- Sophisticated vocabulary, verbs, adjectives
- Phonological awareness
- Rhyme
- Imaginative language

10. *The Lorax* by Dr. Seuss

Dr. Seuss is an author and illustrator powerhouse. His unique style remains unmatched. The rhythm in his books is perfectly measured, and the rhyme and wordplay are superbly designed. The creativity of this book supports whole-brain development, encouraging comparing, contrasting, abstract thinking, problem solving, analysing, forming opinions, etc.

- Wordplay
- Rhyme
- Rhythm

- Comparing/contrasting
- Inferencing and problem solving
- Empathy development

11. *The Bad-Tempered Ladybird* by Eric Carle.

The Bad-Tempered Ladybird is all about a ladybird who picks a fight with increasingly larger animals at one-hour intervals during the day. It is fun and full of great language-learning opportunities. Suitable for 3–8 years.
   Best for:

- Vocabulary: animals
- Concepts: time, size
- Sequencing

Non-fiction books

- Usborne lift-the-flap books
- *My First Book of Irish Mammals* by Juanita Brown
- *Nano: The Spectacular Science of the Very (Very) Small* by Jess Wade and Melissa Castrillon
- *Usborne Big Book of Colours*
- *Little People, Big Dreams* series
- *The Boy Who Drew Birds* by Jacqueline Davies and Melissa Sweet
- *Chickenology* by Barbara Sandri, Francesco Giubblini and Camilla Pintonato

Books for social and emotional development

Children's Books for Wellbeing (PDST, 2020) have a comprehensive list of book recommendations for social and emotional development, and we would recommend this resource for the classroom. Here are some of our favourite books on the topic of social and emotional development:

- *Up and Down* by Oliver Jeffers
- *Tiger-Tiger, Is it True?* by Byron Katie and Hans Wilhelm
- *The Invisible String* by Patricia Karst and Joanne Lew-Vriethoff
- *The Most Magnificent Thing* by Ashley Spires
- *Have You Filled a Bucket Today?* by Carol McCloud and David Messing
- *Take Five* by Niall Breslin and Sheena Dempsey
- *The Paper Dolls* by Julia Donaldson and Rebecca Cobb
- *The Scarecrows' Wedding* by Julia Donaldson and Axel Scheffler
- *All the Ways To Be Smart* by Davina Bell and Allison Colpoys

- *The Dot* by Peter H. Reynolds
- *Only a Tree Knows Wow To Be a Tree* by Mary Murphy

Books that support inclusion and diversity

- *I Talk Like a River* by Jordan Scott and Sydney Smith
- *The Paper Bag Princess* by Robert Munsch and Michael Martchenko
- *The Smeds and the Smoos* by Julia Donaldson and Axel Scheffler

Books for the first day at school

- *Owl Babies* by Martin Waddell and Patrick Benson
- *The Kissing Hand* by Audrey Penn, Ruth E. Harper and Nancy M. Leak

Books for speech and language therapy

Books are a great tool for SLTs. Below is a list of therapy targets and books which are useful. Of course, these are just examples and you can build your own library of books for use in therapy. Once you become familiar with the books, you will find that a good-quality book will be useful for a wide variety of therapy targets.

Vocabulary development

Animals:

- *Brown Bear, Brown Bear, What Do You See?* by Bill Martin Jnr and Eric Carle
- *All Afloat on Noah's Boat* by Tony Mitton and Guy Parker-Rees
- *Giraffes Can't Dance* by Giles Andreae and Guy Parker-Rees
- *Monkey Puzzle* by Julia Donaldson and Axel Scheffler
- *The Bad-Tempered Ladybird* by Eric Carle
- *The Smartest Giant in Town* by Julia Donaldson and Axel Scheffler
- *What the Ladybird Heard* by Julia Donaldson and Axel Scheffler
- *The Highway Rat* by Julia Donaldson and Axel Scheffler

Food:

- *The Very Hungry Caterpillar* by Eric Carle
- *The Lighthouse Keeper's Lunch* by Ronda and David Armitage
- *The Tiger Who Came to Tea* by Judith Kerr

Vehicles:

- *Amazing Aeroplanes, Terrific Trains, Roaring Rockets, Super Submarines*, series of Books by Tony Mitton and Ant Parker

- *Goodnight Tractor* by Michelle Robinson and Nick East
- *Goodnight, Goodnight, Construction Site* by Sherri Duskey Rinker and Tom Lichtenheld
- *Look Inside: Things That Go* by Rob Lloyd Jones and Stefano Tognetti
- *Cars, Trucks and Things That Go* by Richard Scarry

Clothes:

- *The Smartest Giant in Town* by Julia Donaldson and Axel Scheffler
- *We Wear Pants* by Katie Abey
- *Hippo Has a Hat* by Julia Donaldson and Nick Sharratt

Early verbs:

- *It's a Little Baby* by Julia Donalson and Rebecca Cobb
- *The Giant Jumperee* by Julia Donaldson and Helen Oxenbury

Concepts:

- *That's Not My...* series by Fiona Watt and Rachel Wells
- *Dear Zoo* by Rod Campbell (big, tall, grumpy, scary)
- *The Lion's Share* by Matthew McElligott (half, middle, quarter, twice)
- *Different? Same!* by Heather Tekavec and Pippa Curnick

Grammar

Regular past tense:

- *Marvin Gets Mad* by Joseph Theobald
- *The Detective Dog* by Julia Donaldson and Sara Ogilvie
- *Owl Babies* by Martin Waddell and Patrick Benson
- *Alfie* series by Shirley Hughes

Irregular past tense:

- *Room on the Broom* by Julia Donaldson and Axel Scheffler
- *Zog* by Julia Donaldson and Axel Scheffler
- *The Bad-Tempered Ladybird* by Eric Carle

Pronouns:

- *Alfie* series by Shirley Hughes
- *Pip and Posy* series by Axel Scheffler

- *Rosie Revere* series by Andrea Beaty and David Roberts
- *Room on the Broom* by Julia Donaldson and Axel Scheffler

Phonological awareness

Rhyming books:

- *Ten Little Fingers and Ten Little Toes* by Mem Fox and Helen Oxenbury
- Julia Donaldson books
- *The Cat in the Hat* by Dr. Seuss and many more books by the same author which have superb rhyme and wordplay
- *Demolition* by Sally Sutton and Brian Lovelock
- *Rosie Revere, Engineer* by Andrea Beaty and David Roberts. Also: *Iggy Peck, Architect* and *Ada Twist, Scientist*
- *My Friend Bear* by Jez Alborough
- *Peepo* by Janet and Allan Ahlberg. Also: *Each Peach Pear Plum*
- *The Wonky Donkey* by Craig Smith and Katz Cowley
- *Mother Goose's Nursery Rhymes* by Axel Scheffler

Syllabification:

- *The Very Hungry Caterpillar* by Eric Carle
- *Goodnight Tractor* by Michelle Robinson and Nick East
- *Rosie Revere, Engineer* by Andrea Beaty and David Roberts
- *Demolition* by Sally Sutton and Illustrated by Brian Lovelock

Speech sounds

These books will be very useful when targeting the production of speech sounds in therapy. Books are particularly helpful in generalisation of speech sound targets.

P:

- *Peepo* by Janet and Allan Ahlberg
- *Pip and Posy* by Axel Scheffler
- *Peck, Peck, Peck* by Lucy Cousins
- Nursery rhymes: 'Pat a Cake', 'Two Little Dicky Birds', 'Miss Polly had a Dolly'

T:

- *The Tiger Who Came to Tea* by Judith Kerr
- *Tiddler: The Story-Telling Fish* by Julia Donaldson and Axel Scheffler
- *Terrific Trains* by Tony Mitton and Ant Parker

- *Superworm* by Julia Donaldson and Axel Scheffler
- Nursery Rhymes: 'Head, Shoulders, Knees and Toes', 'I'm a Little Teapot'

K:

- *Cat's Cookbook* by Julia Donaldson and Axel Scheffler
- *Cave Baby* by Julia Donaldson and Emily Gravett
- *Cool Cars* by Tony Mitton and Ant Parker
- *We're Going on a Bear Hunt* by Michael Rosen and Helen Oxenbury
- Nursery Rhymes: 'Polly Put the Kettle On', 'Humpty Dumpty'

B:

- *We're Going on a Bear Hunt* by Michael Rosen and Helen Oxenbury
- *My Friend Bear* by Jez Alborough
- *Dear Zoo* by Rod Campbell
- Nursery rhymes: 'Baa, Baa, Black Sheep', 'BINGO'

D:

- *The Detective Dog* by Julia Donaldson and Sara Ogilvie
- *The Hospital Dog* by Julia Donaldson and Sara Ogilvie
- *Green Eggs and Ham* by Dr. Seuss
- *Hairy Maclary from Donaldson's Dairy* by Lynley Dodd

G:

- *Good Night, Gorilla* by Peggy Rathman
- *Goodnight Moon* by Margaret Wise Brown and Clement Hurd
- *Goodnight Digger* by Michelle Robinson and Nick East
- *We're Going on a Bear Hunt* by Michael Rosen and Helen Oxenbury
- *The Go-Away Bird* by Julia Donaldson and Catherine Rayner

F:

- *The Gruffalo* by Julia Donaldson and Axel Scheffler
- *One Fish, Two Fish, Red Fish, Blue Fish* by Dr Seuss
- *Ten Little Fingers and Ten Little Toes* by Mem Fox and Helen Oxenbury
- Nursery rhymes: 'One Two Three Four Five', 'London Bridge Is Falling Down'

S:

- *Brown Bear, Brown Bear, What Do You See?* by Bill Martin Jnr and Eric Carle
- *Fox's Socks* by Julia Donaldson and Axel Scheffler

- *Super Submarines* by Tony Mitton and Ant Parker
- *Dear Zoo* by Rod Campbell
- Nursery Rhymes: 'Six Little Ducks', 'A Sailor went to Sea'

L:

- *What the Ladybird Heard* by Julia Donaldson and Axel Scheffler
- *The Lighthouse Keeper's Lunch* by David and Rhonda Armitage
- *Brown Bear, Brown Bear, What Do You See?* by Bill Martin Jnr and Eric Carle
- *The Snail and the Whale* by Julia Donaldson and Axel Scheffler (L word final position)
- Nursery rhymes: 'Mary had a little lamb'

Sh:

- *Sheep in a Jeep* by Nancy Shaw and Margot Apple
- *Shh! We have a Plan* by Chris Haughton
- *Hooray for Fish!* by Lucy Cousins
- *A Squash and a Squeeze* by Julia Donaldson and Axel Scheffler

R:

- *Rosie Revere, Engineer* by Andrea Beaty and David Roberts
- *Rude Ramsay and the Roaring Radishes* by Margaret Atwood
- *Ribbit Rabbit Robot* by Victoria Mackinlay and Sofya Karmazina
- *Room on the Broom* by Julia Donaldson and Axel Scheffler

M:

- *Marvin Gets Mad* by Joseph Theobald
- *Hairy Maclary from Donaldson's Dairy* by Lynley Dodd
- Nursery rhymes: 'Row, Row, Row, Your Boat', 'Five Little Monkeys'

Ch:

- *Room on the Broom* by Julia Donaldson and Axel Scheffler
- *The Gruffalo's Child* by Julia Donaldson and Axel Scheffler
- *There's a Bear on My Chair* by Ross Collins

J:

- *The Smartest Giant* in Town by Julia Donaldson and Axel Scheffler
- *Giraffes Can't Dance* by Giles Andreae and Guy Parker-Rees

- *The Giant Jumperee* by Julia Donaldson and Helen Oxenbury
- Nursery rhymes: 'Jack and Jill'

Wordless picture books that we love

- *Good Night, Gorilla* by Peggy Rathman
- *One Frog Too Many* by Marianna Mayer and Mercer Mayer
- *Flotsam* by David Wiesner
- *Good Dog Carl* by Alexander Day
- *Rosie's Walk* by Pat Hutchins
- *Journey* by Aaron Becker
- *Chalk* by Bill Thompson
- *Pancakes for Breakfast* by Tomie dePaola
- *Hug* by Jez Alborough
- *The Lion and the Mouse* by Jerry Pinkney

Recommended online resources

- www.talkingbuddies.ie
- www.talknua.com
- www.radld.org
- www.hanen.org
- www.readingrockets.org
- www.thebabblingbookclub.com
- www.childrensbooksireland.ie
- www.bookfairypantryproject.org
- www.librariesireland.ie

Conclusion

We can make a positive difference to the language environment by sharing books and getting the most out of them to support speech and language development.

Books are a tangible tool and are easily accessed by most people in society. Irrespective of whether books are shared for the purpose of language development or simply for pleasure, every read-aloud session will expose children to new vocabulary and much more. Books offer the opportunity to explore different perspectives, opinions, problems and solutions. For speech and language therapists, books are an invaluable tool to use in the clinic for language development. If we can get the message out there that all children should hear stories read aloud every day, we would give children a great gift. In the words of Jim Trelease, 'it's not the toys in the house that make the difference in children's lives, it's the words in their heads. The least expensive thing we can give a child outside of a hug turns out to be the most valuable: words' (Trelease & Giorgis, 2019). In the classroom, books can play a central role, offering an anchor point and a context for all types of learning. With the ever-growing push for technology and screen-based learning in our society, prioritising quality face-to-face interactions with picture books has never been more of a priority.

Read to Me!

Read to me, mammy, read stories each day,
it's never too early to start, so they say,
read stories of dragons and ladybirds and frogs,
of Gruffalos, giants and big fluffy dogs

Read to me, daddy, I just long to hear
stories of places far away from here,
stories of magical lands and times,
stories with fun and stories with rhymes

DOI: 10.4324/9781003262961-9

Read to me, sister, you know what it means,
it's time spent together away from the screens,
reading together all cuddled and cosy
will help to make memories that are beautifully rosy

Read to me, brother, read anywhere,
read in the car, on the couch, on the stair,
read in the garden, the bath and the bed,
tell me a story you've made up in your head

Read to me, granny, even when we're apart,
I know you love stories and you read from the heart,
call me and read me a story or two,
I'll listen in and pretend I'm right beside you

Read to me, grandad, about our big world,
read stories of nature and fern fronds unfurled,
read stories of tractors, volcanos and birds,
cause kids who hear stories know lots of words

Read to me, teacher, read to us all,
read to the children, the big and the small,
inspire a love of books by sharing stories every day
because the gift of reading can't be taken away

Remember I'm never too young or too old
to enjoy the pleasure of a story being told

References and bibliography

Bryan, K., Garvani, G., Gregory, J. & Kilner, K. (2015) Language difficulties and criminal justice: The need for earlier identification. *International Journal of Language and Communication Disorders, 50*(6), 763-775. doi:10.1111/1460-6984.12183

Bus, A.G. & van IJzendoorn, M.H. (1999). Phonological awareness and early reading: A meta-analysis of experimental training studies. *Journal of Educational Psychology, 91*(3), 403-414. doi:10.1037/0022-0663.91.3.403

Centre for Early Childhood Development & Education (2006) *Síolta, The National Quality Framework for Early Childhood Education*. Dublin: CECDE.

Ceren Simsek, Z. & Isıkoglu Erdogan, N. (2015). Effects of the dialogic and traditional reading techniques on children's language development. *Procedia - Social and Behavioral Sciences, 197*, 754-758.

Chetty, R. & Hendren, N. (2018). The impacts of neighborhoods on intergenerational mobility I: Childhood exposure effects. *The Quarterly Journal of Economics, 133*(3), 1107-1162. doi:10.1093/qje/qjy007

Cox Gurdon, M. (2019). The Enchanted Hour: The Miraculous Power of Reading Aloud in the Age of Distraction. London: Piatkus.

Department for Education (2013). National curriculum in England. www.gov.uk/government/collections/national-curriculum

Department for Education (2014). *Early Years Foundation Stage Profile: Handbook 2014*. London: Standards & Testing Agency. https://assets.publishing.service.gov.uk/government/uploads/system/uploads/attachment_data/file/301256/2014_EYFS_handbook.pdf

Dickinson, D.K., Griffith, J.A., Golinkoff, R.M. & Hirsh-Pasek, K. (2012). How reading books fosters language development around the world. *Child Development Research, 2012*, Article ID 602807. doi:10.1155/2012/602807

Dixon, J.A. & Marchman, V.A. (2007). Grammar and the lexicon: Developmental ordering in language acquisition. *Child Development, 78*(1), 190-212.

Dr. Seuss (2019). *I Can Read with My Eyes Shut*. London: HarperCollins.

Droegemueller, M. (2019). The importance of nursery rhymes in literacy development. Rolling Prairie Readers. https://rollingprairiereaders.com/importance-of-nursery-rhymes

Ehri, L.C., Nunes, S.R., Stahl, S.A. & Willows, D.M. (2001). Systematic phonics instruction helps students learn to read: Evidence from the National Reading Panel's meta-analysis. American Educational Research Association, 71, 3. doi:10.3102/00346543071003393

Farah, R., Meri, R., Kadis, D.S., Hutton, J., DeWitt, T. & Horowitz-Kraus, T. (2019). Hyperconnectivity during screen-based stories listening is associated with lower narrative comprehension in preschool children exposed to screens vs dialogic reading: An EEG study. *PLoS ONE, 14*(11), e0225445. doi:10.1371/journal.pone.0225445

Gascoigne, M. (2006). Supporting children with speech, language and communication needs within integrated children's services. Royal College of Speech & Language Therapists Position Paper. London: RCSLT.

Gillam, R.B., & Ukrainetz, T.A. (2006). Language intervention through literature-based units. In T.A. Ukrainetz (Ed.), Contextualized Language Intervention: Scaffolding PreK-12 Literacy Achievement (pp.59-94). Pro-Ed Inc.

Grøver, V., Rydland, V., Gustafsson, J.-E. and Snow, C.E. (2020). Shared book reading in preschool supports bilingual children's second-language learning: A cluster-randomized trial. *Child Development, 91*(6), 2192–2210. doi:10.1111/cdev.13348

Hart, B. & Risley, T.R. (1995). *Meaningful Differences in the Everyday Experience of Young American Children*. Baltimore, MD: Brookes.

Hart, B. & Risley, T.R. (2003). The early catastrophe: The 30 million word gap by 3 years. *American Educator, 27*(1), 4–9.

Horst, J.S., Parsons, K.L. & Bryan, N.M. (2011). Get the story straight: Contextual repetition promotes word learning from storybooks. *Frontiers in Psychology*. doi:10.3389/fpsyg.2011.00017

Hutton, J.S., Dudley, J., Horowitz-Kraus T., DeWitt, T. & Holland, S.K. (2020). Associations between screen-based media use and brain white matter integrity in preschool-aged children. *JAMA Pediatrics, 174*(1), e193869. doi:10.1001/jamapediatrics.2019.3869

Jain, V.G., Kessler, C., Lacina, L., Szumlas, G.A., Crosh, C., Hutton, J.S., Needlman, R. & Dewitt, T.G. (2021). Encouraging Parental reading for high-risk neonatal intensive care unit infants. *Journal of Pediatrics, 232*, 95–102. doi:10.1016/j.jpeds.2021.01.003

Jones, J. & Zotovich, K. (2014). Two Peas Comprehensive Phonological Awareness Assessment. www.sess.ie/sites/default/files/Temp_Upload_Files/2014-15/8%20Pg%20PhonologicalAwarenessAssessmentAFoundationalReadingSkillsDiagnosticTool.pdf

Kessler, C., Lacina, L., Szumlas, G.A., Crosh, C., Hutton J.S., Needlman, R. & Dewitt, T.G. (2021). Encouraging parental reading for high-risk neonatal intensive care unit infants. *Journal of Pediatrics, 232*, 95–102. doi:10.1016/j.jpeds.2021.01.003

Kurtts, S.A. & Gavigan, K.W. (2008). Understanding (dis)abilities through children's literature. *Education Libraries, 31*(1). doi:10.26443/el.v31i3.259

Lindfors, R.-M. (2016). Silent Books: A Handbook on Wordless Picture Books Packed with Narrative Power. IBBY Sweden. www.ibby.org/fileadmin/user_upload/Silent_Books_ENG.pdf

Lyytinen, H., Erskine, J., Hämäläinen, J., Torppa, M. & Ronimus, M. (2015). Dyslexia – Early identification and prevention: Highlights from the Jyväskylä Longitudinal Study of Dyslexia. *Current Developmental Disorders Reports, 2*(4), 330–338. doi:10.1007/s40474-015-0067-1

Mackenzie, S. (2018). *The Read-Aloud Family. Making Meaningful and Lasting Connections with Your Kids*. Grand Rapids, MI: Zondervan.

Malcomess, K. (2019). Course notes: Care Aims.

Montag, J., Jones, M. & Smith, L. (2015). The words children hear: Picture books and the statistics for language learning. *Psychological Science, 26*(9). doi:10.1177/0956797615594361

Nation, K., Dawson, N.J. & Hsiao, Y. (2022). Book language and its implications for children's language, literacy and development. *Current Directions in Psychological Science, 31*(4). doi:10.1177/09637214221103264

National Council for Curriculum and Assessment (NCCA) (2009). *Aistear: The Early Childhood Curriculum Framework*. Dublin: NCCA.

National Council for Curriculum and Assessment (2019). *Primary Languages Curriculum*. Dublin: NCCA.

National Early Literacy Panel (2008). *Developing Early Literacy: Report of the National Early Literacy Panel*. Jessup, MD: NELP. www.pathstoliteracy.org/wp-content/uploads/2022/04/NELPReport09.pdf

National Reading Panel (2000). *Teaching Children to Read: An Evidence-Based Assessment of the Scientific Research Literature on Reading and Its Implications for Reading Instruction*. www.nichd.nih.gov/publications/pubs/nrp/smallbook

Neri, E., De Pascalis, L., Agostini, F., Genova, F., Biasini, A., Stella, M. & Trombini, E. (2021). Parental book-reading to preterm born infants in NICU: The effects on language development in the first two years. *International Journal of Environmental Research and Public Health, 18*(21), 11361. doi:10.3390/ijerph182111361

Nippold, M.A., Mansfield, T.C., Billow, J.L. & Tomblin, J.B. (2008). Expository discourse in adolescents with language impairments: Examining syntactic development. *American Journal of Speech and Language Pathology, 17*(4), 356–366. doi:10.1044/1058-0360(2008/07-0049)

Organisation for Economic Cooperation and Development (2002). *Reading for Change: Performance and Engagement Across Countries. Results from PISA 2000*. Paris: OECD.

Oxford English Dictionary (2023). Vocabulary. Oxford Languages. https://languages.oup.com/dictionaries/#oed

Paul, P. & Russo, M. (2019). *How to Raise a Reader*. New York, NY: Workman Publishing Company.

Pepper, J., & Weitzman, E. (2004). *It Takes Two to Talk: A practical guide for parents of children with language delays*. (2nd ed.). Toronto: The Hanen Centre.

Phonological Awareness Working Group (2019). *Demonstration Project on In-school and Early Years Therapy Support*. Ireland: NCSE.

Professional Development Services for Teachers (2020). *Children's Books for Wellbeing*. Dublin: PDST.

Pugh, K. (2014). Embracing dyslexia: The Interviews – Dr. Ken Pugh. *YouTube*. www.youtube.com/watch?v=xACBr9BusRM

Ramsey, W.R., Bellom-Rohrbacher, K. & Saenz, T. (2021). The effects of dialogic reading on the expressive vocabulary of pre-school aged children with moderate to severely impaired expressive language skills. *Child Language Teaching and Therapy*, 37(3), 279–299. doi:10.1177/02656590211019449

Scarborough, H.S. (2001). Connecting Early Language and Literacy to Later Reading (Dis)abilities: Evidence, Theory, and Practice. In S. Neuman & D. Dickinson (Eds.), *Handbook for Research in Early Literacy* (pp.97–110). New York, NY: Guilford Press.

Schuele, C.M. & Boudreau, D. (2008). Phonological awareness intervention: Beyond the basics. *Language, Speech, and Hearing Services in Schools*, 39(1), 3–20. doi:10.1044/0161-1461(2008/002)

Schwab, J.F. & Lew-Williams, C. (2016). Language learning, socioeconomic status, and child-directed speech. *Wiley Interdisciplinary Reviews: Cognitive Science*, 7(4), 264–275. doi:10.1002/wcs.1393

Simsek, Z.C. & Erdogan, N.I. (2015). Effects of the dialogic and traditional reading techniques on children's language development. *Procedia: Social and Behavioural Sciences*, 197, 754–758.

Sláintecare (2019) *Sláintecare Action Plan 2019*. Dublin: Department of Health.

Sosa, A.V. (2016) Association of the type of toy used during play with the quantity and quality of parent-infant communication. *JAMA Pediatrics*, 170(2), 132–137. doi:10.1001/jamapediatrics.2015.3753

Stephan, T. (2016). Oh, those questions?! Hanen Early Language Program. The Hanen Centre. www.hanen.org/SiteAssets/Helpful-Info/Articles/oh-those-questions---printer-friendly.aspx

Talktime (2019). Classroom Strategies. Compiled by Demonstration Project of In School Therapy and Early Years Therapy supports. NCSE, Ireland.

Trelease, J. & Giorgis, C. (2019). *Jim Trelease's Read-Aloud Handbook*, 8th Edition. New York, NY: Penguin Books.

Vygotsky, L.S. (1978). *Mind in Society: The Development of Higher Psychological Processes*. Cambridge, MA: Harvard University Press.

Wanzek, J., Dickson, S., Bursuck, W.D. & White, J.D. (2000). Teaching phonological awareness to students at risk for reading failure: An analysis of four instructional programs. *Learning Disabilities Research and Practice*, 15(4), 226–239. doi:10.1207/SLDRP1504_6

Wasik, B.A. & Bond, M.A. (2001). Beyond the pages of a book: Interactive book reading and language development in preschool classrooms. *Journal of Educational Psychology*, 93(2), 243–250. doi:10.1037/0022-0663.93.2.243

Watkins, P. (2018). Extensive reading for primary in ELT. Part of the Cambridge Papers in ELT series. Cambridge: Cambridge University Press. www.cambridge.org/us/files/7915/7488/5311/CambridgePapersInELT_ExtReadingPrimary_2018_ONLINE.pdf

Weisleder, A. & Fernald, A. (2013). Talking to children matters: Early language experience strengthens processing and builds vocabulary. *Psychological Science*, 24(11), 2143–2152.

Wesseling, P.B.C., Christmann, C.A. & Lachmann, T. (2017). Shared book reading promotes not only language development, but also grapheme awareness in German kindergarten children. *Journal of Frontiers in Psychology*. https://doi.org/10.3389/fpsyg.2017.00364

Wiesner, D. (2021). Talk at the opening of exhibition entitled 'Speechless: The Art of Wordless Picture Books', Eric Carle Museum of Picture Book Art, Amherst, MA.

Woldmo, R. (2019). Phonological awareness: An instructional and practical guide for use in the kindergarten classroom. www.uwo.ca/fhs/lwm/teaching/dld_2018_19/Woldmo_PAGuideKindergarten.pdf

Zauche, L.H., Thul, T.A., Mahoney, A.E.D. & Stapel-Wax, J.L. (2016). Influence of language nutrition on children's language and cognitive development: An integrated review. *Early Childhood Research Quarterly*, 36, 318–333. doi:10.1016/j.ecresq.2016.01.015

Appendices

Appendix 1

Two Peas Comprehensive Phonological Awareness Test

Two Peas Phonological Awareness Assessment

Name_____ Date_____ Teacher_____ Grade_____

1-Counting Words in a Spoken Sentence
"How many words are in this sentence?" (w/ chips)

___ ___ ___ Ben likes books. (3)
___ ___ ___ I have one toy. (4)
___ ___ ___ Where is my bag? (4)
___ ___ ___ What's the big deal? (4)
___ ___ ___ Annie likes to play games. (5)
___ ___ ___ Tomorrow is Saturday. (3)
BOY MOY EOY

__/6 __/6 __/6 **Total** (App.A)

2-Rhyme Recognition
"Give me a thumbs-up if these are rhyming words."

___ ___ ___ fuzzy/wuzzy (yes)
___ ___ ___ cold/hot (no)
___ ___ ___ lamp/stamp (yes)
___ ___ ___ bless/guess (yes)
___ ___ ___ tape/pen (no)
___ ___ ___ pink/wink (yes)
BOY MOY EOY

__/6 __/6 __/6 **Total** (K.RFS.2a)

3-Rhyme Production
*"What rhymes with ___?"*Record student responses.
Accept real& nonsense words.

___ ___ ___ take   _____
___ ___ ___ pig   _____
___ ___ ___ hill   _____
___ ___ ___ right   _____
___ ___ ___ nice   _____
___ ___ ___ mail   _____
BOY MOY EOY

__/6 __/6 __/6 **Total** (K.RFS.2a)

4-Single Syllable Onset-Rime Blending
"What word is this?"

___ ___ ___ b-ird (bird)
___ ___ ___ n-ight (night)
___ ___ ___ sl-eep (sleep)
___ ___ ___ r-ing (ring)
___ ___ ___ f-ace (face)
___ ___ ___ sl-ime (slime)
BOY MOY EOY

__/6 __/6 __/6 **Total** (K.RFS.2c)

5-Single Syllable Onset-Rime Segmenting
"Say the first part (onset) and then the last part (rime)."

___ ___ ___ land (l-and)
___ ___ ___ watch (w-atch)
___ ___ ___ dream (dr-eam)
___ ___ ___ big (b-ig)
___ ___ ___ noise (n-oise)
___ ___ ___ club (cl-ub)
BOY MOY EOY

__/6 __/6 __/6 **Total** (K.RFS.2c)

6-Syllable Blending & Pronouncing
"What word is this ___ - ___?"

___ ___ ___ back-pack (backpack)
___ ___ ___ cook-ies (cookies)
___ ___ ___ pen-cil (pencil)
___ ___ ___ wel-come (welcome)
___ ___ ___ ham-bur-ger (hamburger)
___ ___ ___ air-plane (airplane)
BOY MOY EOY

__/6 __/6 __/6 **Total** (App.A)

7-Syllable Segmenting & Counting
"Say the parts of each word. How many parts do you hear?"

___ ___ ___ butterfly (3)
___ ___ ___ glasses (2)
___ ___ ___ magnet (2)
___ ___ ___ watermelon (4)
___ ___ ___ dragonfly (3)
___ ___ ___ blanket (2)
BOY MOY EOY

__/6 __/6 __/6 **Total** (K.RFS.2b)

8-Phoneme Alliteration & Discrimination
"Which word has a different first sound?"

___ ___ ___ wise, wacky, <u>friend</u>, woman
___ ___ ___ rope, <u>fly</u>, runt, rooster
___ ___ ___ juice, joke, jelly, <u>fox</u>
___ ___ ___ moon, milk, movie, <u>paper</u>
___ ___ ___ <u>light</u>, phone, fence, field
___ ___ ___ tub, tent, <u>bear</u>, tooth
BOY MOY EOY

__/6 __/6 __/6 **Total** (App.A)

9-Phoneme Isolation of Initial Sounds
"What is the first sound in this word?"

___ ___ ___ pinch (p)
___ ___ ___ wish (w)
___ ___ ___ football (f)
___ ___ ___ house (h)
___ ___ ___ zipper (z)
___ ___ ___ summer (s)
BOY   MOY   EOY

__/6 __/6 __/6 **Total** (K.RFS.2d, 1.RFS.2c)

10-Phoneme Isolation of Final Sounds
"What is the last sound in this word?"

___ ___ ___ baseball (l)
___ ___ ___ street (t)
___ ___ ___ fox (x)
___ ___ ___ home (m)
___ ___ ___ wind (d)
___ ___ ___ rag (g)
BOY   MOY   EOY

__/6 __/6 __/6 **Total** (K.RFS.2d, 1.RFS.2c)

11-Phoneme Isolation of Medial Sounds
"What's the middle sound in this word?" (1st) Is it long or short?"

___ ___ ___ game /ai/ (long)
___ ___ ___ rib /i/ (short)
___ ___ ___ beak /ee/ (long)
___ ___ ___ night /ie/ (long)
___ ___ ___ fog /o/ (short)
___ ___ ___ tub /u/ (short)
BOY   MOY   EOY

__/6 __/6 __/6 **Total** (K.RFS.2d, 1.RFS.2a, 2c)

12-Phoneme Blending
"What word do these sounds make?"

___ ___ ___ /g//u//m/ (gum)
___ ___ ___ /s//o//ck/ (sock)
___ ___ ___ /g//e//s//t/ (guest)
___ ___ ___ /t//ee//th/ (teeth)
___ ___ ___ /d//r//ie//v/ (drive)
___ ___ ___ /s//t//a//n//d/ (stand)
BOY   MOY   EOY

__/6 __/6 __/6 **Total** (K.RFS.2d, 1.RFS.2b)

13-Phoneme Segmenting
"Tell me the sounds in the word ____." (w/ chips)

___ ___ ___ play (/p//l//ay/)
___ ___ ___ junk (/j//u/n//k/)
___ ___ ___ ripple (/r//i//p//l/)
___ ___ ___ snack (/s//n//a//ck/)
___ ___ ___ wonder (/w//u//n//d//r/)
___ ___ ___ cabin (/c//a//b//i//n/)
BOY   MOY   EOY

__/6 __/6 __/6 **Total** (K.RFS.2d, 1.RFS.2d)

14-Phoneme Addition
"Lay. Add /p/ to the beginning of lay? What's the word?"

___ ___ ___ tar, add /s/ (star)
___ ___ ___ ink, add /w/ (wink)
___ ___ ___ all, add /b/ (ball)
___ ___ ___ cream, add /s/ (scream)
___ ___ ___ lake, add /f/ (flake)
___ ___ ___ rain, add /g/ (grain)
BOY   MOY   EOY

__/6 __/6 __/6 **Total** (K.RFS.2e, 1.RFS.2b)

15-Phoneme Substitution
"Rope. Change /r/ to /s/. What's the new word?"

___ ___ ___ hop, change /h/ to /p/
___ ___ ___ best, change /b/ to /r/
___ ___ ___ wiggle, change /w/ to /g/
___ ___ ___ ramp, change /r/ to /l/
___ ___ ___ hand, change /h/ to /s/
___ ___ ___ park, change /p/ to /d/
BOY   MOY   EOY

__/6 __/6 __/6 **Total** (K.RFS.2e, 1.RFS.2b)

16-Phoneme Deletion
"Say ____. Say____ without the /__/."

___ ___ ___ smartie, without the /s/ (-martie)
___ ___ ___ flower, without the /f/ (-lower)
___ ___ ___ horse, without the /h/ (-orse)
___ ___ ___ bunny, without the /b/ (-unny)
___ ___ ___ doctor, without the /d/ (-octor)
___ ___ ___ ranch, without the /r/ (-anch)
BOY   MOY   EOY

__/6 __/6 __/6 **Total** (App. A)

Notes:

Source: ©2014 Hello Two Peas Comprehensive Phonological Awareness Assessment www.hellotwopeasinapod.com

Appendix 2

How to select a good children's book

HOW TO SELECT A
GOOD CHILDREN'S BOOK

Good range of words and interesting vocabulary	Detailed illustrations	Interactive/ sensory books
Story has rhyme and rhythm	Story promotes empathy/ inclusion/ diversity	Engaging/ fun/ interesting story
Story has lots of repetition	You enjoy reading this book	Book matches your child's interests/ seasonal topics

Figure 5.1

Appendix 3
Cheat sheets

STORY OF THE WEEK: Cheat Sheet	Targets:
Date: **Title/Author/Illustrator:** *The Snail and the Whale* by Julia Donaldson and Axel Scheffler **Themes:** Adventure, friendship, kindness ***Curriculum Links:*** *Aistear. Oral Language Curriculum*	
Vocabulary *(Strand Unit 5: Vocabulary)* • **Nouns:** Whale, soot, trail, tide, iceberg, dolphin, parrot, turtle, monkey, palm trees, fins, lighthouse, cave, shark, volcano, flock, shore, tide • **Verbs:** Slithered, gazed, long, sniffed, wriggle, hitch, shimmering, spray, foamed, arched, flashing, zigging, zooming, upsetting, beached, squirting • **Adjectives:** Immensely, enormous, hideous, vast, pale	
Concepts: *(Strand Unit 8: Categorisation)* **Basic concepts:** big, small, cool **Prepositions:** in, on	
Grammar: *(Strand Unit 4: Sentence Structure and Grammar)* • **Pronouns:** 'I' • **Regular past tense:** gazed, carried, crashed • **Irregular past tense:** came, said, stuck, held, swam, lost, told, sang	
Inferencing and Problem Solving: *(Strand Unit 12: Description Prediction and Reflection)* • The other snails don't want to go away from their rock. I wonder why. • I wonder how the snail was feeling when the whale held out his tail. Did you ever feel like that? • I wonder how the whale was feeling when he was stuck on the sand. • How was the snail feeling as he approached the school?	

Phonological Awareness *(Reading: Strand Unit 4: Phonological and Phonemic Awareness)*
 	
• **Rhyme:** Every sentence contains rhyme: sighed/wide, rock/dock, sail/snail
• **Segmentation:** Break words into parts:
  ○ 2 syllable words: slith-ered, Ice-berg, moun-tain
  ○ 3 syllable words: hid-e-ous, feath-er-y, sil-ver-y, imm-ens-ely, e-nor-mous, won-der-ful,
  ○ Sentences: 'lift wanted around the world' (5 words)
  ○ Compound words: hump-back, star-lit, thunder-storm, zig-zag, speed-boat	

STORY OF THE WEEK: Cheat Sheet	Targets:
Date: **Title/Author/Illustrator:** *Rosie Revere, Engineer* by Andrea Beaty and David Roberts **Theme:** Creative thinking, determination, resilience **Curriculum Links:** Aistear (Communicating). Oral language curriculum	
Vocabulary *(Strand Unit 5: Vocabulary)* • **Nouns:** engineer, trash, stash, treasures, helium, pythons, eaves, attic, lever, dawn, invention, cockpit • **Verbs:** daring, peeking, swooping, grew sleepy, chuckled, wheezed, lingers, hauled, sputtered, whirled, froze • **Adjectives:** shy, proud, embarrassed, perplexed, dismayed, ridiculous, baffle	
Concepts: *(Strand Unit 8: Categorisation)* **Basic concepts:** Young/old, alone, high **Prepositions:** in, under,	
Grammar: *(Strand Unit 4: Sentence Structure and Grammar)* • **Pronouns:** She • **Regular past tense:** dreamed, peeked, finished, looked, approached, hauled _____ • **Irregular past tense:** sat, flew, built, made, grew, hid, knew, stuck, kept, froze, thought	
Open questions to encourage discussion: *(Strand Unit 12: Description Prediction and Reflection)* 1. I wonder why she didn't want anyone to see her machines. 2. Do you think helium pants are a good idea? 3. Have you ever invented anything? 4. Fred said he liked the cheese hat, but he was laughing… I wonder why.	
Phonological Awareness: *(Reading: Strand Unit 4: Phonological and Phonemic Awareness)* **Rhyming words:** Revere, engineer, cheer, tears, clear **Syllable Segmentation:** • 2 Syllable words: Ro-sie, mo-ment, giz-mo, sputt-er, fail-ure • 3 Syllable words En-gin-eer, he-li-um, in-ven-tion, dy-na-mo • 6 syllable: hel-i-o-cheese-cop-ter **Compound Words:** hot-dog, hide-away, zoo-keeper, every-one, heart-beat, cock-pit	

STORY OF THE WEEK: Cheat Sheet	Targets:
Date: Title/Author/Illustrator: *The Very Hungry Caterpillar* by Eric Carle Theme: Food, metamorphosis Curriculum Links: Aistear (Communicating). Oral Language Curriculum	
Vocabulary *(Strand Unit 5: Vocabulary)* • **Nouns:** (person, place, thing) Food vocabulary: apple, pear, watermelon, plum, strawberry, orange, pickle, swiss cheese, salami, ice cream cone Caterpillar, butterfly, cocoon • **Verbs:** (action words) Pop, ate, pushed • **Adjectives:** (describing words) Hungry	
Concepts: *(Strand Unit 8: Categorisation)* • **Basic concepts:** Tiny, warm, still, little, big, small, more than • **Prepositions:** On the leaf, through,	
Grammar: *(Strand Unit 4: Sentence Structure and Grammar)* • **Pronouns** (Examples: he, she, I, me, they, them, him, her) He • **Regular past tense**: (Examples: walk**ed**, jump**ed**) Started, pushed • **Irregular past tense**: Examples: flew, ate, thought, drive, sang) Ate, came	
Open questions to encourage discussion: *(Strand Unit 12: Description Prediction and Reflection)* 1. I wonder why he feels better after eating the leaf. 2. Do you think caterpillars would really eat lollipops? 3. What kids of foods make you feel good/bad?	
Phonological Awareness *(Reading: Strand Unit 4: Phonological and Phonemic Awareness)* • **Segmentation:** Break words into parts: ○ 2 syllable words: hung-ry, co-coon, app-le, or-ange, cup-cake, pick-le ○ 3 syllable words: straw-berr-y, lol-i-pop, choc-o-late, sal-a-mi, butt-er-fly ○ 4 syllable words: wa-ter-mel-on, cat-er-pill-ar ○ Compound Words: Cup-cake, water-melon	

STORY OF THE WEEK: Cheat Sheet	Targets:
Date: **Title/Author/Illustrator:** *Zog* by Julia Donaldson and Axel Scheffler **Theme:** Friendship, kindness, success, failure **Curriculum Links:** Aistear (Communicating). Oral Language Curriculum	
Vocabulary *(Strand Unit 5: Vocabulary)* • **Nouns:** dragon, champion, throat, bandage, fumes, career, knight, stethoscope, ambulance • **Verbs:** soared, swooped, practise, crashed, zigzagged, twirled, captured, prancing, implore • **Adjectives:** sticky, gleaming, hoarse, soothing, wildly, resounding, fearsome	
Concepts: *(Strand Unit 8: Categorisation)* • **Basic concepts:** young, old, high, low, biggest, smallest, loud, quiet	
Grammar: *(Strand Unit 4: Sentence Structure and Grammar)* • **Pronouns:** he, she, his, you, mine • **Regular past tense:** tried, crashed, twirled • **Irregular past tense:** flew, grew, blew, taught, fell, ran, won	
Open questions to encourage discussion: *(Strand Unit 12: Description Prediction and Reflection)* 1. I wonder how Zog felt when he couldn't do the things he wanted. How will he get better at blowing fire? Flying? 2. I wonder what else Pearl had in her bag. Let's look at our first aid kit... 3. I wonder why Pearl doesn't like being a princess. 4. Would you like to be a princes/prince? Why?	
Phonological Awareness *(Reading: Strand Unit 4: Phonological and Phonemic Awareness)* • **Rhyme:** far, star; own, grown; free, tree; flew, blue • **Segmentation:** Break words into parts: ○ 2 syllable words: dra-gon, prin-cess, res-cue, fri-lly, bon-fires, ban-dage ○ 3 syllable words: gad-a-bout, steth-o-scope, re-sound-ing, cham-pi-on, pepp-er-mint. Ex-cell-ent ○ 4 syllable: tem-per-a-ture	

STORY OF THE WEEK: Cheat Sheet	Targets:
Date: **Title/Author/Illustrator:** *The Dinky Donkey by Craig Smith and Katz Cowley* **Theme:** *Animal* **Curriculum Links:** *Aistear. Oral Language Curriculum*	
Vocabulary *(Strand Unit 5: Vocabulary)* **Nouns:** Donkey, child, girl, eyelashes, hooves, music, piano, sunglasses **Verbs:** Paints, loved, listen, wore, play **Adjectives:** wonky, dinky, winky, little, cute, small, beautiful, long, blinky, inky, pinky, punky, rowdy, plinky plonky, wild, funky, stinky	:
Concepts: *(Strand Unit 8: Categorisation)* **Basic concepts:** little/small/dinky, big, long	
Grammar: *(Strand Unit 4: Sentence Structure and Grammar)* • **Pronouns:** she • **Regular past tense:** loved • **Irregular past tense:** wore, smelt	
Phonological Awareness: *(Reading: Strand Unit 4: Phonological and Phonemic Awareness)* **Rhyming words**: wonky, donkey, dinky, winky, blinky, inky, pinky, plinky plonky, funky, stinky **Syllable Segmentation:** • 2 syllable words: row-dy, listen, paint-ed • 3 syllable words: beaut-i-ful, pi-an-o, eye-lash-es, sun-glass-es • Sentences: 'it was a little girl' (5 words) • Compound words: sun-glasses, eye-lashes	

Appendix 3
Cheat sheet template

STORY OF THE WEEK: Cheat Sheet	Targets:
Date: **Title/Author/Illustrator:** **Theme:** **Curriculum Links:** *Aistear*. **Oral Language Curriculum**	
Vocabulary *(Strand Unit 5: Vocabulary)* • **Nouns:** (person, place, thing) _____ • **Verbs:** (action words) _____ • **Adjectives:** (describing words) _____	
Concepts: *(Strand Unit 8: Categorisation)* **Basic concepts:** (Examples: big/small, full/empty, long/short, wet/dry, hot/cold, same/different) **Prepositions:** (Examples: on, in, under, in front, behind, between, beside) _____	
Grammar: *(Strand Unit 4: Sentence Structure and Grammar)* • **Pronouns** (Examples: he, she, I, me, they, them, him, her) _____ • **Regular past tense**: (Examples: walk**ed**, jump**ed**) _____ • **Irregular past tense**: (Examples: flew, ate, thought, drive, sang) _____ • **Plurals:** (Examples: cat**s**, dog**s**, crayon**s**) _____ • **Irregular plurals** (Examples: mice, teeth, geese, men) _____	

Open questions to encourage discussion: *(Strand Unit 12: Description Prediction and Reflection)*
   1.
   2.
   3.	

Phonological Awareness: *(Reading: Strand Unit 4: Phonological and Phonemic Awareness)* **Rhyming words**: _____ _____ **Syllable Segmentation:** • 2 Syllable words: _____ • 3 Syllable words: _____ • 4 syllable words: _____ **Compound Words:** _____	

Appendix 4

How picture books can target all areas of the oral language curriculum

Book: The Snail and the Whale by Julia Donaldson and Axel Scheffler Theme: Beach		
Element	Learning Outcome	Through appropriately playful learning experiences, children should be able to:
Communicating	1. Engagement, listening and attention	Child shows interest in the book and can sustain joint attention. Child can actively attend and engage with the story.
	2. Motivation and choice	Child will listen to and respond to the text for pleasure and interest
	3. Social conventions and awareness of others	Child will sustain interest in the topic and engage in conversations using appropriate social communication skills.
Understanding	4. Sentence Structure and Grammar	Child will hear grammar of increasing length and complexity with regular and irregular past tense, complex compound sentences and conjunctions.
	5. Vocabulary	Child will be exposed to new vocabulary: Whale, soot, trail, tide, iceberg, dolphin, parrot, turtle, monkey, palm trees, fins, lighthouse, cave, shark, volcano, flock, shore, tide. Immensely, enormous, hideous, vast, pale.
	6. Demonstration of Understanding	Demonstration of understanding by analysing how the snail can help the whale.
Exploring and using	7. Requests and questions	• Answers open questions relating to the story: The other snails don't want to go away from their rock. I wonder why? • I wonder how the snail was feeling when the whale held out his tail. Did you ever feel like that? • I wonder how the whale was feeling when he was stuck on the sand. • How was the snail feeling as he approached the school?
	8. Categorisation	Child can name, describe and categorise object related to the beach and animal themes. For example, animals that live in the water vs. animals that live in the air. Vehicles that are used for rescuing vs transport.
	9. Retelling and elaborating	Child can retell the sequence of the narrative with support. Child can talk about a picture scene and retell and elaborate on what he notices about the picture.

(Continued)

(Continued)

Book: *The Snail and the Whale by Julia Donaldson and Axel Scheffler* Theme: *Beach*		
Element	*Learning Outcome*	*Through appropriately playful learning experiences, children should be able to:*
	10. Playful and creative use of language	Child will be exposed to a variety of descriptive verbs and reflect on how the words sound like what they say: Slithered, gazed, long, sniffed, wriggle, hitch, shimmering, spray, foamed, arched, flashing, zigging, zooming, upsetting, beached, squirting.
	11. Information giving, explanation and justification	Child will discuss the strategy for saving the whale and what could be done differently.
	12. Description, prediction and reflection	Child will reflect on the story and predict different outcomes

Appendix 5

Rainbow Oral Language Programme themes (Fallon) and suggested picture books to match

Junior infants

Month	Oral Language Development Yearly Plan	Suggested picture books
September	○ First Day at School	○ *The Kissing Hand* by Audrey Penn, Ruth E. Harper and Nancy M. Leak ○ *Owl Babies* by Martin Waddell and Patrick Benson ○ *The Invisible String* by Patricia Karst and Joanne Lew-Vriethoff ○ *Come to School Too, Blue Kangaroo* by Emma Chichester Clark
	○ At the Doctor's	○ *Zog* by Julia Donaldson and Axel Scheffler ○ *How your Body Works* (Usborne) ○ *Zog and the Flying Doctors* by Julia Donaldson and Axel Scheffler ○ *Hospital Dog* by Julia Donaldson and Sara Ogilvie
October	○ Autumn	○ *The Squirrels Who Squabbled* by Rachel Bright and Jim Field ○ *The Little Red Hen* by Paul Galdone ○ *Autumn* by Gerda Muller ○ *Pumpkin Soup* by Helen Cooper ○ *Leaf Man* by Lois Ehlert
	○ Halloween	○ *Room on the Broom* by Julia Donaldson and Axel Scheffler ○ *What's in the Witch's Kitchen?* by Nick Sharratt ○ *Meg and Mog* by Helen Nicoll and Jan Pieńkowski ○ *Gustavo the Shy Ghost* by Flavia Z. Drago ○ *Winnie the Witch* series By Valerie Thomas and Korki Paul ○ (*Winnie's Amazing Pumpkin*)
November	○ At the Restaurant	○ *The Tiger Who Came to Tea* by Judith Kerr ○ *Mrs Wobble the Waitress* by Janet and Allan Ahlberg
December	○ Santa's Workshop	○ *Stick Man* by Julia Donaldson and Axel Scheffler ○ *The Jolly Postman* by Janet and Allan Ahlberg
January	○ A Rainy Day	○ *On a Magical Do-Nothing Day* by Beatrice Alemagna ○ *All Afloat on Noah's Boat* by Tony Mitton and Guy Parker-Rees
	○ At the Airport	○ *Amazing Aeroplanes* by Tony Mitton and Ant Parker

(Continued)

(Continued)

Month	Oral Language Development Yearly Plan	Suggested picture books
February	○ In the Morning	○ *Farmer Duck* by Martin Waddell and Helen Oxenbury
	○ On the Farm	○ *The Great Irish Farm Book* by Darragh McCullough and Sally Caulwell ○ *What the Ladybird Heard* by Julia Donaldson and Axel Scheffler ○ *Rosie's Walk* by Pat Hutchins ○ *Farming* by Gail Gibbons
March	○ Up in the Treehouse	○ *Stuck* by Oliver Jeffers ○ *The Koala Who Could* by Rachel Bright and Jim Field
	○ The Arctic	○ *Elliot's Artic Surprise* by Catherine Barr and Francesca Chessa ○ *Wolf in the Snow* by Matthew Cordell
April	○ The Jungle	○ *Giraffe's Can't Dance* by Giles Andreae and Guy Parker-Rees ○ *Different? Same!* by Heather Tekavec and Pippa Curnick
May	○ The Pet Shop ○ The Supermarket	○ *When the Dragons Came* by Naomi Kefford, Lynne Moore and Benji Davies ○ *Off to the Market* by Alice Oehr ○ *The Tiger Who Came to Tea* by Judith Kerr ○ *Maisy Goes Shopping* by Lucy Cousins
June	○ The Seaside	○ *What the Ladybird Heard at the Seaside* by Julia Donaldson and Axel Scheffler ○ *Sharing a Shell* by Julia Donaldson and Lydia Monks ○ *Pip and Posy: The New Friend* by Axel Scheffler ○ *Look What I Found at the Seaside* by Moira Butterfield and Jesús Verona

Senior infants

Month	Oral Language Development Yearly Plan	
September	○ The Birthday Party	○ *Alfie and the Birthday Surprise* by Shirley Hughes ○ *Alfie Gives a Hand* by Shirley Hughes ○ Postman Bear (*Tales from Acorn Wood*) by Julia Donaldson and Axel Scheffler ○ *Kipper's Birthday* by Mick Inkpen
	○ Space	○ *Usborne Book of Space* ○ *The Smeds and the Smoos* by Julia Donaldson and Axel Scheffler ○ *The First Hippo on the Moon* by David Walliams and Tony Ross ○ *Roaring Rockets* by Tony Mitton and Ant Parker

(Continued)

Month	Oral Language Development Yearly Plan	
October	○ Fun at the Fair	○ *Alfie Wins a Prize* by Shirley Hughes
	○ Halloween on Haunted Hill	○ *Spookyrumpus* by Tony Mitton and Guy Parker-Rees
November	○ The School Yard	○ *Alfie and the Big Boys* by Shirley Hughes
	○ The Post Office	○ *The Jolly Postman* by Janet and Allan Ahlberg
December	○ The Ice Rink (Christmas)	○ *The Polar Express* by Chris Van Allsburg ○ *The Gruffalo's Child* by Julia Donaldson and Axel Scheffler
January	○ Antarctica	○ *365 Penguins* by Jean Luc-Fromental and Joëlle Jolivet ○ *Little People Big Dreams: Ernest Shackelton* by Maria Isabel Sanchez Vegara and Olivia Holden ○ *Lost and Found* by Oliver Jeffers ○ *Penguin* by Polly Dunbar ○ *Geronimo* By David Walliams and Tony Ross ○ *The Penguin Who Wanted to Find Out* by Jill Tomlinson
	○ The Cinema	○ *Maisy Goes to the Cinema* by Lucy Cousins
February	○ The Garden Centre (Spring)	○ *The Night Gardener* by Terry and Eric Fan ○ *Grandpa's Garden* by Stella Fry and Sheila Moxley ○ *GIYs Know It All Allmanac* by Michael Kelly, Muireann Ní Chíobháin and Fatti Burke ○ *Oliver's Vegetables* by Vivian French and Alison Bartlett ○ *Pip and Egg* by Alex Latimer and David Litchfield ○ *A Seed Is Sleepy* by Dianna Hutts Aston and Sylvia Long ○ *Yucky Worms* by Vivien French and Jessica Ahlberg
March	○ Vets	○ *The Hospital Dog* by Julia Donaldson and Sarah Ogilvie ○ *Mrs Vole the Vet* by Allan Ahlberg ○ *Hairy McClary's Rumpus at the Vet* by Lynley Dodd ○ *Construction* by Sally Hutton and Brian Lovelock
	○ The Library	○ *The Dog Detective* by Julia Donaldson and Sarah Ogilvie
April	○ The DIY Store	○ *What We'll Build* by Oliver Jeffers
May	○ The Circus	○ *Peter Spier's Circus!* by Peter Spier ○ *The Singing Mermaid* by Julia Donaldson and Axel Scheffler
	○ Home Sweet Home	○ *The Paper Dolls* by Julia Donaldson and Rebecca Cobb ○ *Meerkat Mail* by Emily Gravett ○ *Peace at Last* by Jill Murphy ○ *Where the Wild Things Are* by Maurice Sendak ○ *Peck Peck Peck* by Lucy Cousins ○ *Peepo!* by Janet and Allan Ahlberg
June	○ We're Going to the Zoo	○ *Usborne Peep Inside the Zoo* by Anna Milbourne and Simona Dimitri ○ *The Lion's Share* by Matthew McElligott ○ *Gorilla* by Anthony Browne ○ *The Dead Zoo* by Peter Donnelly ○ *Dear Zoo* by Rod Campbell ○ *1, 2, 3 to the Zoo* by Eric Carle

Appendix 6

Reading picture books at home:
Information sheets for caregivers

8 benefits of reading aloud to your child

1. Reading supports the child's brain development. Brain scans clearly show how the child's brain develops and grows as they hear stories read aloud.
2. Reading aloud supports attention and listening skills. Attention and listening develop page by page, book by book.
3. Reading aloud develops the child's understanding of language concepts such as first, last, before, after, above, below.
4. Reading aloud promotes vocabulary development as children hear new words that do not come up in everyday conversation. Vocabulary development is associated with later academic success.
5. Reading aloud promotes phonological awareness which is an important pre-literacy skill and sets children up for later reading success.
6. Reading aloud teaches empathy as every time a child hears a story, they take a walk in someone else's shoes.
7. Reading aloud helps a child to develop higher-level language skills such as problem solving, inferencing and predicting.
8. Reading aloud is a quality quiet time to spend with your child away from screens and the busyness of daily life.

Top tips for reading aloud to your child

1. Slow down when reading aloud. Read slowly enough for the child to form pictures in their head.
2. Talk about the picture. Quality picture books have amazing illustrations that have so much to talk about, and it is in these little conversations that language development gets a turbo boost!
3. Resist the temptation to bombard your child with too many questions. Comment on what you see and wait for your child to have a turn.
4. Ask open questions to help your child to think beyond the book. These are questions that begin with the phrase 'I wonder...'
5. Relate new words to your child's everyday experience. Talk about new words lots and let your child hear you using these new words in conversation.

6. Repeat the same book lots. Research shows that repeating the same book has great benefits for language development.
7. Select quality picture books to read aloud. Some books are better than others for language development. Check out www.talkingbuddies.ie for recommendations.
8. Make reading aloud part of your daily routine.

Book recommendations for children aged 0-2

1. *Faces* by Baby Focus: First Touch
   This book is for brand-new babies to help develop their eyesight. It includes a variety of high-contrast black, white and yellow faces. There is also a mirror at the end so baby can look and smile at their own reflection.

2. *Mother Goose's Nursery Rhyme Book* by Axel Scheffler
   This delightful collection of nursery rhymes is illustrated by the extremely talented Axel Scheffler. His illustrations have great success in keeping children engaged and getting the conversation flowing. This book is suitable for children aged 0-5 years.

3. *Where's Spot?* by Eric Hill
   Where's Spot? is a much-loved classic. This book is great for developing understanding of prepositions in a fun and interactive way; the lift-the-flap feature is sure to keep children engaged.

4. *First 100 Board Book Box Set* (three books) by Roger Priddy
   A simple yet effective book. Ideal for exposure to basic vocabulary targets. Brightly illustrated with images of real objects rather than cartoons! Photograph and written word underneath every image. Ideal for children aged 0-2 years.

5. *That's Not My...* book series by Fiona Watts and Rachel Wells
   This gorgeous book series is aimed at very young children. Brilliant bright pictures are sure to gain their attention. The patches of different textures support sensory development. The repetitive language in this book is ideal for new talkers!

6. *Peepo!* by Janet and Allan Ahlberg
   This book is simply magical. There is so much detail in these illustrations, offering plenty of opportunity for language development. Children aged 0-4 years can benefit from the wide range of vocabulary in this book. The rhyming text is great for supporting phonological awareness. The interactive feature and the predictable, repetitive storyline in this book keep toddlers engaged.

7. *Dear Zoo* by Rod Campbell
   This book is appropriate for children aged 1-3 years. Its bright colours and lift-the-flap features help gain and keep attention and engagement. The repetitive storyline and array of concepts is great for toddlers! Check our other books by Rod Campbell such as *Dear Santa*, *It's Mine* and *Oh Dear*.

8. *Each Peach Pear Plum* by Janet and Allan Ahlberg
   This enchanting book is filled with many nursery rhyme references. The illustrations in this book are visually rich and detailed. Children will love spotting all the hidden details in the pictures and be sure to get a conversation going about everything happening in this book.

9. *Ten little fingers and Ten Little Toes* by Mem Fox and Helen Oxenbury

   There are few things sweeter than tiny baby fingers and toys. This book is simply charming, and you will love reading it as much as sharing it with your little one. This book is filled with gorgeous illustrations. The rhyming, repetitive text primes young developing brains with the foundations for learning to read. The sense of belonging as you shift through the pages celebrates babies of different ethnicities and cultures from around the world.

10. *Tickle* by Leslie Patricelli

    This brightly coloured book is a fun way to engage little ones. Nice simple illustrations and a great way to talk about body parts.

11. *Polar Bear, Polar Bear, What Do You Hear?* By Bill Martin Jr and Eric Carle

    This book is designed to help toddlers tune in their ears to identify and hear wild animals and the sounds they make.

Book recommendations for children aged 2–3 years

1. *Postman Bear* by Julia Donaldson and Axel Scheffler
   This charming book is part of the Acorn Woods series and it has beautiful illustrations, interactive lift-the-flaps and a nice strong structure which supports narrative development. Check out the other books in the series also such as *Fox's Socks*, *Rabbit's Nap* and *Hide-and-Seek Pig*.

2. *Mr. Brown Can Moo, Can You?* by Dr. Seuss
   This classic book is full of silly sounds, rhythm and rhyme. It has lots of repetition and is great fun to read aloud.

3. *The Very Hungry Caterpillar* by Eric Carle
   Another classic book which was first published in 1969. This book has bright, bold illustrations and tells the story of a little caterpillar who eats his way through the book before pupating and turning into a caterpillar.

4. *Monkey Puzzle* by Julia Donaldson and Axel Scheffler
   This clever book tells the story of a little monkey who is searching for his mum in the jungle helped along by a kind butterfly. Suitable for children up to 0–5 years.

5. *We're Going on a Bear Hunt* by Michael Rosen and Helen Oxenbury
   This much-loved book tells the tale of a family adventure. Beautiful illustrations and engaging, repetitive storyline. Suitable for children aged 1–5 years.

6. *Goodnight Digger* by Michelle Robinson and Nick East
   Beautifully illustrated book with repetitive text which is perfect for the bedtime routine.

7. *Peck Peck Peck* by Lucy Cousins
   This is a fabulous, fun, heart-warming book with bright, bold illustrations and interactive holes for little fingers to wiggle through. Suitable for children up to 5 years.

8. *Pip and Posy: The Super Scooter* by Axel Scheffler
   Pip and Posy are two friends who often face a little challenge in their day. In this book, Posy snatches Pip's scooter, but then falls and hurts her knee. There is a whole series of Pip and Posy books and we love them for their simple text and detailed illustrations.

9. *Good Dog Carl* by Alexandra Day
   This is a fun wordless picture which tells the unusual story of Carl, a Rottweiler who takes care of the baby while mom is out.

10. *Cars, Trucks and Other Things That Go* by Richard Scarry
    This is a fun and somewhat outlandish book with detailed magical illustrations on the topic of vehicles. So much to talk about and notice on each page. Perfect for dialogic reading.

11. *Owl Babies* by Martin Waddell and Patrick Benson
This is a story of three baby owls who are nervously waiting for their mother's return. It's a delightfully reassuring story which supports the child who has separation anxiety.

Book recommendations for children aged 3-5 years

1. *The Gruffalo* by Julia Donaldson and Axel Scheffler
   This tale of a clever little mouse who tricks the animals in the wood is world-famous at this stage. It is a fun and engaging story and it's also great for language development. Check out the full range of Julia Donaldson books as they are superb for language development. Other titles include *The Snail and the Whale*, *Superworm*, *The Highway Rat*, *The Detective Dog*, *The Hospital Dog*, *Zog*, *Room on the Broom*, *The Paper Dolls*, *Stick Man*, *The Gruffalo's Child*, *Cave Baby*, *The Smartest Giant in Town*, *A Squash and a Squeeze*, *The Go-Away Bird*.

2. *The Kissing Hand* by Audrey Penn, Ruth E. Harper and Nancy M. Leak
   This is a classic story which is read widely to children to help them prepare for school and the anxieties that often come from separating from loved ones at this time.

3. *One Frog Too Many* by Mariana Mayer and Mercer Mayer
   This wordless picture book tells about the adventures of a little boy and his pets. It explores emotions such as jealousy, sadness, guilt and happiness.

4. *Pig the Pug* by Aaron Blabey
   This is a hilarious story of a greedy dog who won't share his toys.

5. *Marvin Gets Mad* by Joseph Theobald
   Marvin the Sheep explodes with anger when his friend takes his apple. This funny story explores themes of anger and temper tantrums.

6. *Alfie...* book series by Shirley Hughes
   The Alfie book series is a beautifully told set of stories with tales of the simple day-to-day events in Alfie's family. The illustrations are detailed and nostalgic, and cause the reader to look just a little longer. The books explore a variety of themes such as kindness, jealousy, fear, joy and friendship.

7. *Pip and Posy: The Super Scooter* by Axel Scheffler
   Pip and Posy are two friends who often face a little challenge in their day. In this book, Posy snatches Pip's scooter, but then falls and hurts her knee. There is a whole series of *Pip and Posy* books, and we love them for their simple text and detailed illustrations.

8. *Terrific Trains* by Tony Mitton and Ant Parker
   This book is full of rhythmic rhyme and detailed illustrations. The book brings non-fiction to life with information about trains presented in a fun and engaging way. Check out other books in this series including *Tremendous Tractors*, *Dazzling Diggers* and *Super Submarines* for all those vehicle-crazy preschoolers. Suitable for children up to 5 years.

Book recommendations for 5+

1. *The Lion's Share* by Matthew McElligott
   This terrific book tells the tale of a tiny ant who receives an invitation to dine with the lion along with other guests from the jungle. She is shocked by the behaviour of the animals and wants to make it up to the king by baking him a cake. Lots of fun ensues when the other boastful guests turn it into a competition. Unique illustrations.

2. *The Squirrels Who Squabbled* by Rachel Bright and Jim Field
   This is a fun story of two greedy squirrels who find themselves in a race for the last pinecone of the season.

3. The Lorax by Dr. Seuss
   The Lorax is the original eco-warrior and, like all Dr. Seuss books, this is a fun story with lots of wordplay.

4. *On a Magical Do-Nothing Day* by Beatrice Alemagna
   This is a story of a child who feels bored and just wants to play video games all day. When the video game falls into a pond, all seems lost until the world around seems to come alive.

5. *The True Story of the Three Little Pigs* by Jon Scieszka and Lane Smith
   This story tells the tale of the classic three little pigs but from the point of view of the Big Bad Wolf!

6. *The Lighthouse Keeper's Lunch* by Ronda and David Armitage
   This modern classic tells the story of Mr Grinling the lighthouse keeper and his wife who must think of a way to stop the greedy seagulls from stealing the lunch she prepares for him every day.

7. *Rabbit and Bear* by Julian Gough and Jim Field
   Beautifully illustrated, this series of books tells the tale of friendship alongside other themes such as embarrassment, guilt and frustration. More suitable for 6+.

8. *The Smeds and the Smoos* by Julia Donaldson and Axel Scheffler
   This extra-terrestrial story of friendship highlights the importance of diversity and inclusion. No matter what our cultural differences and looks are, they should not separate us. The rhyming text, the vocabulary, the wordplay, the illustrations are all just phenomenal.

9. *The Snail and the Whale* by Julia Donaldson and Axel Scheffler
   This beautifully illustrated book tells the tale of a snail who goes on an adventure on the tail of a whale. This book sends a powerful message of confidence despite size. The rhyming text is superbly orchestrated and coupled with rich vocabulary and detailed illustrations – a winning combination for supporting vocabulary development.

10. *The Wonky Donkey* by Craig Smith and Katz Cowley
    The Wonky Donkey is a hilarious book about a donkey. The rhythm, rhyme and repetitive text keep the attention of children of all ages. There is a surprising higher-level language component, which is great for interpreting and inferring the meaning of words and phrases.

11. *Rosie Revere, Engineer* by Andrea Beaty and David Roberts
    This clever, witty book is a delight to read. The book motivates children to have courage and follow their passions and interests. The creative storyline is filled with fantastic vocabulary, rhyming text and multisyllabic words.

12. *The Lorax* by Dr. Seuss
    Dr Seuss is an author and illustrator powerhouse. His unique style remains unmatched. The rhythm in his books is perfectly measured, and the rhyme and wordplay are superbly designed. The creativity of this book supports whole-brain development; encouraging comparing, contrasting, abstract thinking, problem solving, analysing, forming opinions, etc.

13. *The Bad-Tempered Ladybird* by Eric Carle
    The Bad-Tempered Ladybird is all about a ladybird who picks a fight with increasingly larger animals at one-hour intervals during the day. It is fun and full of great language learning opportunities.

Non-fiction books

- Usborne lift-the-flap books
- *My First Book of Irish Mammals* by Juanita Brown
- *Nano The Spectacular Science of the Very (Very) Small* by Jess Wade and Melissa Castrillon
- *Usborne Big Book of Colours*
- *Little People, Big Dreams* series
- *The Boy Who Drew Birds* by Jacqueline Davies and Melissa Sweet
- *Chickenology* by Barbara Sandri, Francesco Giubblini and Camilla Pintonato

Appendix 7

Noun matrix and adjective matrix

CATEGORY	FUNCTION	PARTS
What group does new word belong to	What does it do? What is it used for?	What parts belong with this word
SENSES	**THE NEW WORD IS**	**PERSONAL EXPERIENCE**
Taste, smell, feels like	_____	Relate to a time That your child has experienced
WHERE DO YOU FIND IT	**LOOKS LIKE**	**ASSOCIATIONS**
e.g. kitchen, outside, Paris	Talk about shape, size, features	what goes with this? e.g toothpaste goes with toothbrush

Figure 3.1 Noun matrix

EXPLAIN THE WORD	PUT IT NEW WORD IN A SENTENCE	ACT IT OUT/ DRAW IT Act out or draw the meaning of the word!
COMPARE THE WORD TO SOMETHING THAT MEANS THE OPPOSITE	THE NEW WORD IS: _____	CHOOSE A WORD THAT MEANS THE SAME AS THE NEW WORD
PERSONAL EXPERIENCE Talk about a time when you experienced this word	ASSOCIATIONS; WHAT DOES THE NEW WORD REMIND YOU OF?	PHON. AWARENESS Clap out the parts to the word

Figure 3.3 Adjective matrix

INDEX